WELCOME

BUZZWORDS & BS

Let's face it, we've all been guilty of "circling back" to "touch base" with a colleague to get a "30,000 foot view" so you can create a "strategic staircase" to pick the "low-hanging fruit."

Stephen Kirlew \ Author.

INTRODUCTION

Okay, so maybe you haven't packed all of those buzzwords into one sentence, but I'm sure you know someone who has. Since 2020 forced many of us to work from home, maybe you've even discovered you're married to a "let's circle back" guy/girl.

I'm Stephen Kirlew and having worked in boardrooms on both sides of the Atlantic, I've come to learn that there's one thing we all have in common: cringeworthy buzzwords!

That's why I've written *'Buzzwords & BS'*, a lighthearted look at business buzzwords. A buzzword lover's (or hater's) bible, if you will.

The book's main character, Bob Sheldon (BS), is, of course, a fictitious character, but he embodies the buzzword-loving company executives (me included) many of us have met during our careers. Give this book to the 'Bob Sheldons' in your life to see how many buzzwords they recognize.

Without further ado, let the "rubber meet the road" and let's get started…

Buzzwords & BS | Stephen Kirlew

BOB SHELDON
A BITESIZE BIOGRAPHY

Born in [censored by Bob Sheldon] **to Bettina, a shark diver, and Bob Sr., a professional liar, Bob's first words were, "You're fired," to his European au pair.**

Although described by his second wife, Moira, as a [censored by Bob Sheldon]**, Bob's parents were in fact married, albeit briefly.**

In High school, Bob was voted 'Most Likely to Marry for Money' by his classmates. He began his acceptance speech with, "We are gathered here today...".

Bob's heroes include his mother for gifting the world with his presence. His favorite pastime is checking his bank account. He is currently writing his autobiography, 'In Bob We Trust'.

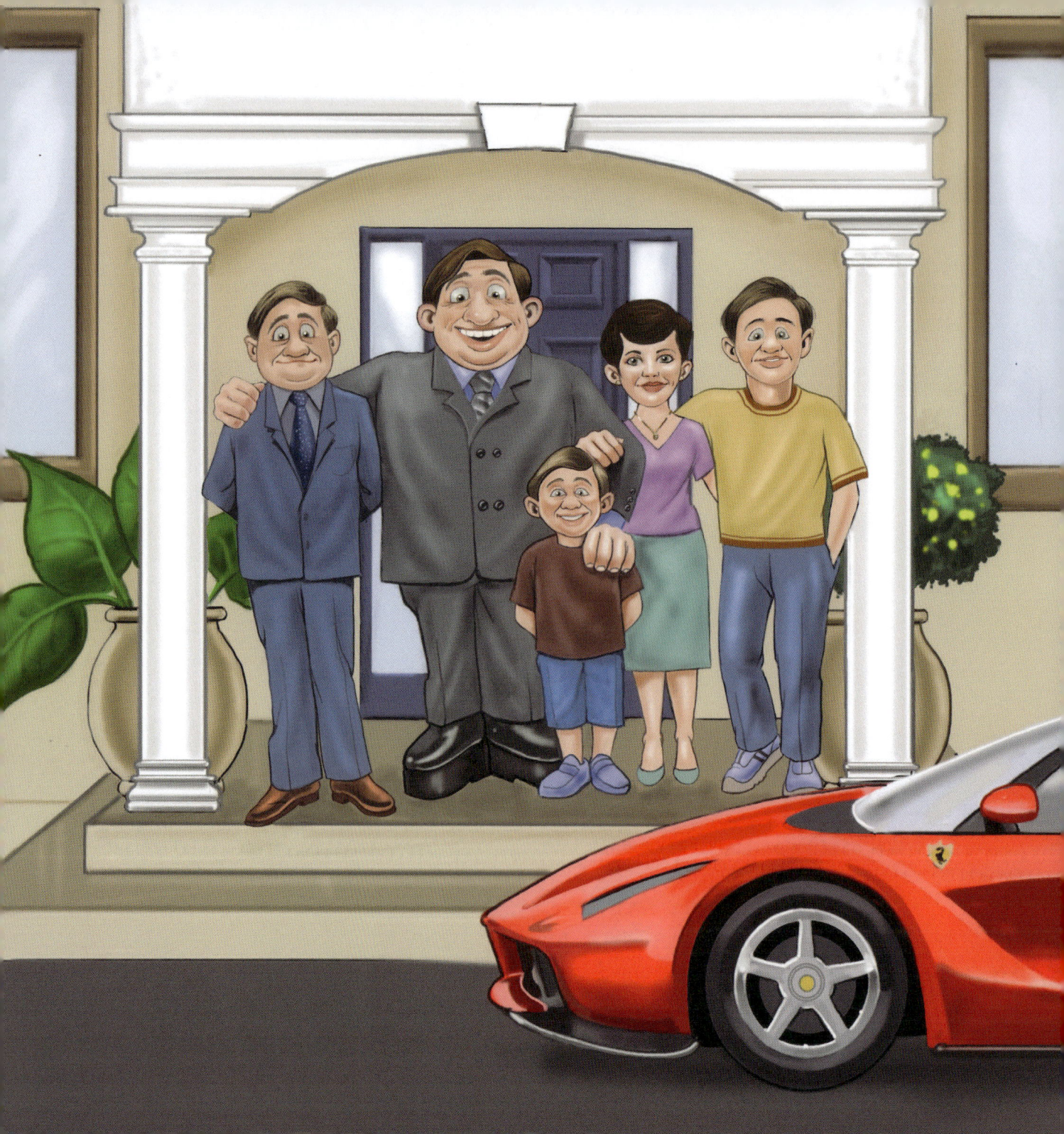

BOB SHELDON
THE VITAL STATISTICS

Age: [Censored by Bob Sheldon]

Birthday: March 8th

Height: 5' 8" - 6' (Editor's note: depending on size of shoe heel)

Weight: 228 lbs ("My muscles are heavy.")

Shoe size: 8 US

Birthplace: [Censored by Bob Sheldon as he is suing the town for refusing to rename itself 'Bobsville']

Self-awareness score: "Self-what?"

IQ score: "Just less than Einstein, much more than Frankenstein."

Marital status: Married to his third wife, Jordana

Children: Three boys—Bob Jnr. III (25) Bob W. Jnr III (17) and Bob H. Jnr III (8)

ACKNOWLEDGEMENTS

What started out as a flippant comment
("This is going to be the title of my first book")
several months ago, has led to what you now hold
in your hands — something I'm pretty proud to be
sharing with you.

I couldn't have done it alone and I have many people
to thank for helping me bring *'Buzzwords & BS'* to life,
none more so than my wonderful wife, Aimee Kirlew.
Aimee, you've supported and believed in me
every step of the way!

Many others have also helped me, including,
but not limited to, the amazing individuals listed here…

Aimee Kirlew
USA
Buzzword #36,
ROADMAP

Andy Barker
UK
Buzzword #40,
SHOW PONY

Austin Roper
USA
Buzzword #39,
SHOTGUN APPROACH

Carl Knudson
USA
Buzzword #13,
DRINKING THE KOOL-AID

Case Hannon
Thailand
Buzzword #24,
IN THE WEEDS

Craig Sanders
UK
Buzzword #45,
STRIKE WHILE THE IRON IS HOT

Danielle Hayes
USA
Buzzword #9,
CIRCLE BACK

Holly Knudson
USA
Buzzword #30,
PEEL BACK THE ONION

Jason Brooks
UK
Buzzword #49,
WHAC-A-MOLE

Jacqeline Compton
USA
Buzzword #35,
PUT TO BED

Joshua Morgan
UK
Buzzword #12
DRINKING FROM THE FIREHOSE

Junior Shelver
South Africa
Buzzword #47,
THROW UNDER THE BUS

Louise Kirlew
UK
Buzzword #18,
FLAVOR OF THE MONTH

Lyman Winn
USA
Buzzword #11,
DEEP DIVE

Martins Lorencis
Latvia
Buzzword #6
BOIL THE OCEAN

Matt Brito
UK
Buzzword #8,
CHANGE AGENT

Nathan Bowles
UK
Buzzword #4,
BEST-IN-CLASS

Royce Hacket
USA
Buzzword #16,
ELEVATOR PITCH

Seth White
USA
Buzzword #25,
LIPSTICK ON A PIG

Sheree Evans
USA
Buzzword #48,
TOUCH BASE

Wendy Frankovich
USA
Buzzword #42,
SOUP TO NUTS

Wes Roper
USA
Buzzword #32,
POST-MORTEM

Buzzwords & BS | Stephen Kirlew

"800-POUND GORILLA"

The Origin

This primate themed phrase is believed to be based on a popular riddle from the 1970s:

'Where does an 800-pound gorilla sleep?

...Anywhere it wants!'

The Meaning

In the business world, an 800-pound gorilla refers to a seemingly undefeatable person or organization that lives by its own rules and defeats competitors with ease.

Bob Sheldon says...

"I know how to defeat the 800-pound gorilla. Get the elephant in the room to sit on it."

Buzzwords & BS | Stephen Kirlew

"30,000 FOOT VIEW"

The Origin
Legend has it that (literally) high-flying company executive, Bob Sheldon, coined this buzzword on a napkin after having a work-related "Eureka!" moment in his first class airplane seat in the mid-1980s.

The Meaning
To give a '30,000 foot view' is to explain something in the style of a pilot's perspective of the world: a high-level overview without the finer details.

Bob Sheldon says...

"Spare me the yawn fest – give me the 30,000 foot view. Like Michelangelo in the Sistine Chapel, I want the big picture."

Buzzwords & BS | Stephen Kirlew

"BANDWIDTH"

The Origin

The term bandwidth has been with us since the 19th century. First, in relation to broadcast radio, and now data transfers, such as when I provide my followers with updates about my life on Facebook, Instagram, Twitter and YouTube.

Oh, and Pinterest, Tik Tok and Tumblr.

The Meaning

This business buzzword is used to describe the resources needed (such as time and effort) to complete a project.

Bob Sheldon says...

" Slow bandwidth? Do I download tomorrow's Investor Report or this--ahem--business-critical image? No contest. Vrrrm! Vrrrm! "

015

Buzzwords & BS | Stephen Kirlew

"BEST-IN-CLASS"

The Origin
This buzzword probably originates from the world's greatest dog show, Crufts, where a visiting Bob Sheldon thought the canine categorization could translate to his staff members.

The Meaning
Although this cliché is used to compliment someone for being a high performer, this proverbial 'good dog' pat on the head is somewhat patronizing.

Bob Sheldon says...

" Last year Nathan was best-in-class. This year he needs a pooper scooper. "

Buzzwords & BS | Stephen Kirlew

"BITE THE BULLET"

The Origin
It's believed this phrase alludes to the practice of literally clenching a bullet in your teeth to cope with the pain of surgery without anesthetic. (Personally, I prefer anesthetic…)

The Meaning
In a business context, to 'bite the bullet' is to endure an impending, unpleasant situation, like getting your expenses submitted.

Bob Sheldon says…

"How dare you ask me to bite the bullet, Wendy! Do you have any idea how much my pearly-white porcelain veneers cost?"

Buzzwords & BS | Stephen Kirlew

"BOIL THE OCEAN"

The Origin

The true origin of this phrase is as murky as the depths of the Atlantic, but it's believed that it was 'Oklahoma's favorite son', humorist Will Rogers' witty reply to how to defeat the German U-boats in World War I.

The Meaning

To call someone out for attempting to 'boil the ocean' is to criticize them for turning a simple task into a complicated, near impossible task.

Bob Sheldon says...

" There's no need to boil the ocean here, Martins. I only wanted a cup of coffee. "

Buzzwords & BS | Stephen Kirlew

"BOOTS ON THE GROUND"

The Origin
US General Volney F. Warner coined this phrase in a 1980 interview with the Christian Science Monitor to discuss the ground troops who were actively fighting in a military campaign.

The Meaning
Thankfully, there's no fighting involved when this buzzword is used in a business context. It's simply a dramatic way of referring to employees working off-site or a specific location.

Bob Sheldon says...

"Me on boots on the ground duty?! Not in these Italian leather loafers!"

Buzzwords & BS | Stephen Kirlew

"CHANGE AGENT"

The Origin

Historically the term 'change agent' has been used to describe the likes of Martin Luther King and Nelson Mandela who inspired positive societal and cultural changes.

The Meaning

In a business setting, a 'change agent' is someone (either internal or external) who champions and introduces new processes within an organization.

Bob Sheldon says...

"No, Matt, changing the toner in the photocopier doesn't make you a change agent."

Buzzwords & BS | Stephen Kirlew

"CIRCLE BACK"

The Origin
My first attempt at tracing the origins of this buzzword proved fruitless so I circled back and discovered that it relates to repeating a task that wasn't completed the first time round.

The Meaning
In corporate surroundings, this buzzword is used to end a meeting or conversation because nothing is being accomplished or agreed upon. To 'circle back' is to arrange another meeting to try and make progress.

Bob Sheldon says...

" Great conversation, Danielle! Let's circle back on that next week. I can squeeze you in between the finance circle back meeting and the HR circle back meeting. "

Buzzwords & BS | Stephen Kirlew

"CLOSE OF PLAY (COP)"

The Origin

This buzzword is borrowed from the sporting world where it indicates the end of a day's action in tennis or cricket. As you may have guessed from the cricket reference, this one originated in the UK.

The Meaning

If you're asked to have something finished by 'close of play' (COP), it's due by the end of that working day. Variations of this buzzword include 'end of play' (EOP), 'close of business' (COB), and 'end of business' (EOB).

Bob Sheldon says...

" I want the CFO's B2B SLA in my inbox ASAP, but definitely by COP... Oh, and BCC the CIO and COO... OK? "

Buzzwords & BS | Stephen Kirlew

"DEEP DIVE"

The Origin
This term has been used since the 16th century in relation to deep-sea diving. (I went on a deep sea diving course once. 'Deep down' it wasn't for me.)

The Meaning
To undertake a 'deep dive' is to plunge into a thorough examination or comprehensive analysis of a subject or topic.

Bob Sheldon says...

" After that deep dive into our projected sales figures, Lyman, I feel seasick. "

Buzzwords & BS | Stephen Kirlew

"DRINKING FROM THE FIREHOSE"

The Origin

One of the earliest references to this buzzword was in the 1989 movie *UHF* where the prize on an imaginary kids' TV show was to drink from the firehose. As you can imagine, the force of the water catapults the 'lucky' winner across the room.

The Meaning

In business jargon, 'drinking from the firehose' means to be overwhelmed with too much work, information, or responsibility.

Bob Sheldon says...

" Don't complain to me about drinking from the firehose, Joshua. I asked for a coffee two hours ago and I'm still waiting. "

033

Buzzwords & BS | Stephen Kirlew

"DRINKING THE KOOL-AID"

The Origin

There's a tragic backstory to this buzzword. In 1978, cult leader Jim Jones ordered over 900 followers to commit suicide by drinking a grape-flavored liquid laced with poison. Apparently, it wasn't actually Kool-Aid but the name stuck.

The Meaning

In the business world, 'Drinking the 'Kool-Aid' means to fully buy into someone's/an organization's beliefs, teachings, or practices.

Bob Sheldon says...

"Wow, I never thought I'd see the day, but you're really drinking the Kool-Aid here, Carl. Drink up!"

Buzzwords & BS | Stephen Kirlew

"DROP IN THE OCEAN"

The Origin

This phrase evolved from a line in the Bible--namely Isaiah 40:15--that refers to a drop in a bucket having little to no impact. Over time, 'bucket' became 'ocean'. That's inflation for you.

The Meaning

In a business sense, this buzzword is often used when talking about money--usually as a way of describing how insignificant an amount is in the grand scheme of things.

Bob Sheldon says...

"My salary may seem a lot, but it's a drop in the ocean compared to my expense account."

Don't **QUACK** Under Pressure!

Buzzwords & BS | Stephen Kirlew

"DUCKS IN A ROW"

The Origin

Possible origins include the way ducklings follow their mothers in a row, the line of ducks found in shooting galleries, and a bowling game with duckpins from the 18th century.

Which one is correct? Duck knows.

The Meaning

In business, to put your 'ducks in a row' is to ensure that enough organization and planning has taken place in order for a project to be successfully completed.

Bob Sheldon says...

"What do you mean put my ducks in a row? HR said I'm not allowed pets in the office anymore."

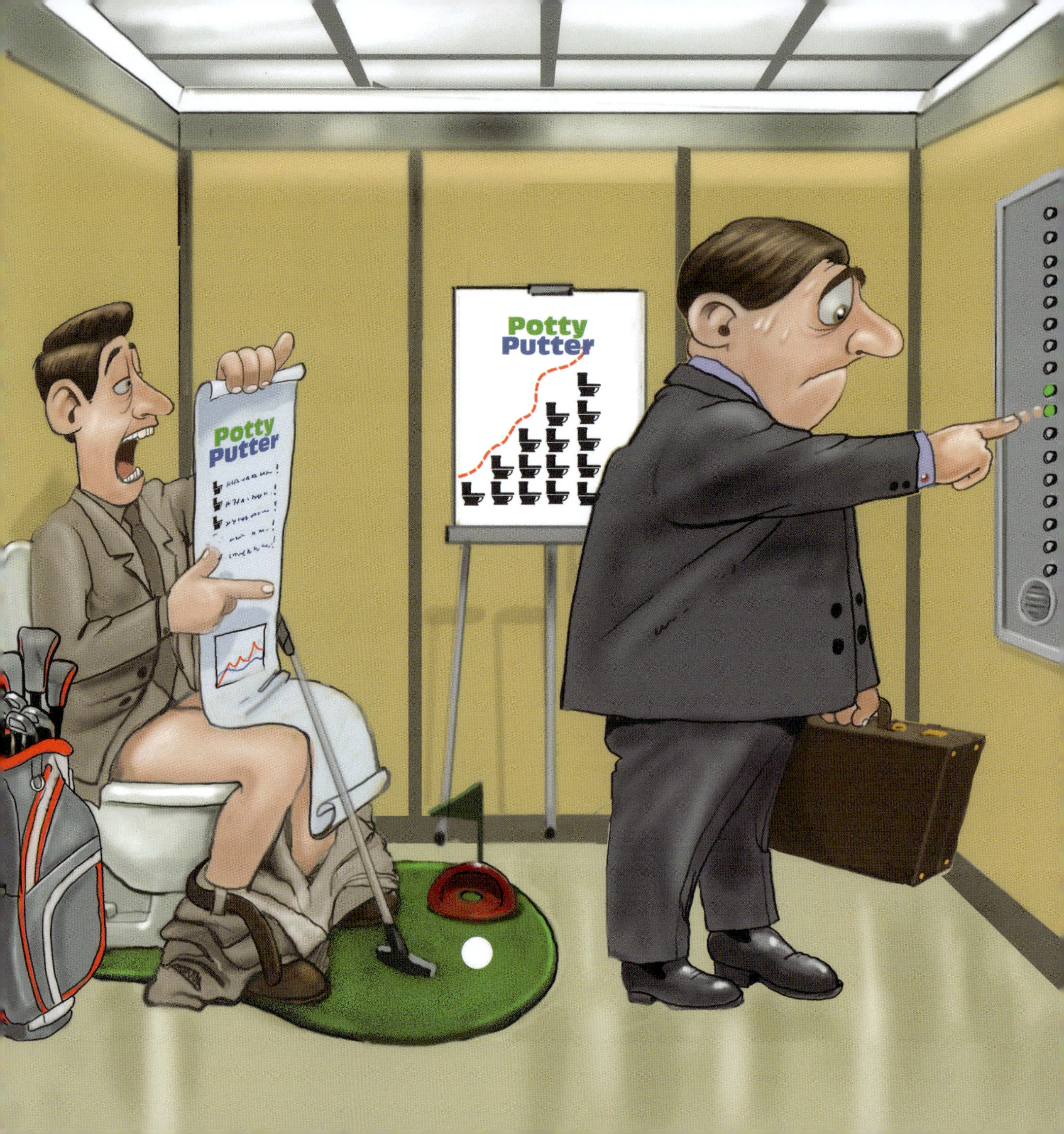
Potty
Putter
Potty
Putter

Buzzwords & BS | Stephen Kirlew

"ELEVATOR PITCH"

The Origin

This buzzword is attributed to businessman and author Philip Crosby who prepared a short speech to deliver to his CEO during an elevator ride. It worked. The impressed CEO invited Crosby to present the full concept to the general managers.

The Meaning

The 'elevator pitch' - a short and succinct summary meant to last no longer than the duration of an elevator ride - is perfect for the business world, a sector where time is money.

Bob Sheldon says...

"Based on your last elevator pitch, Royce... I think I'll take the stairs."

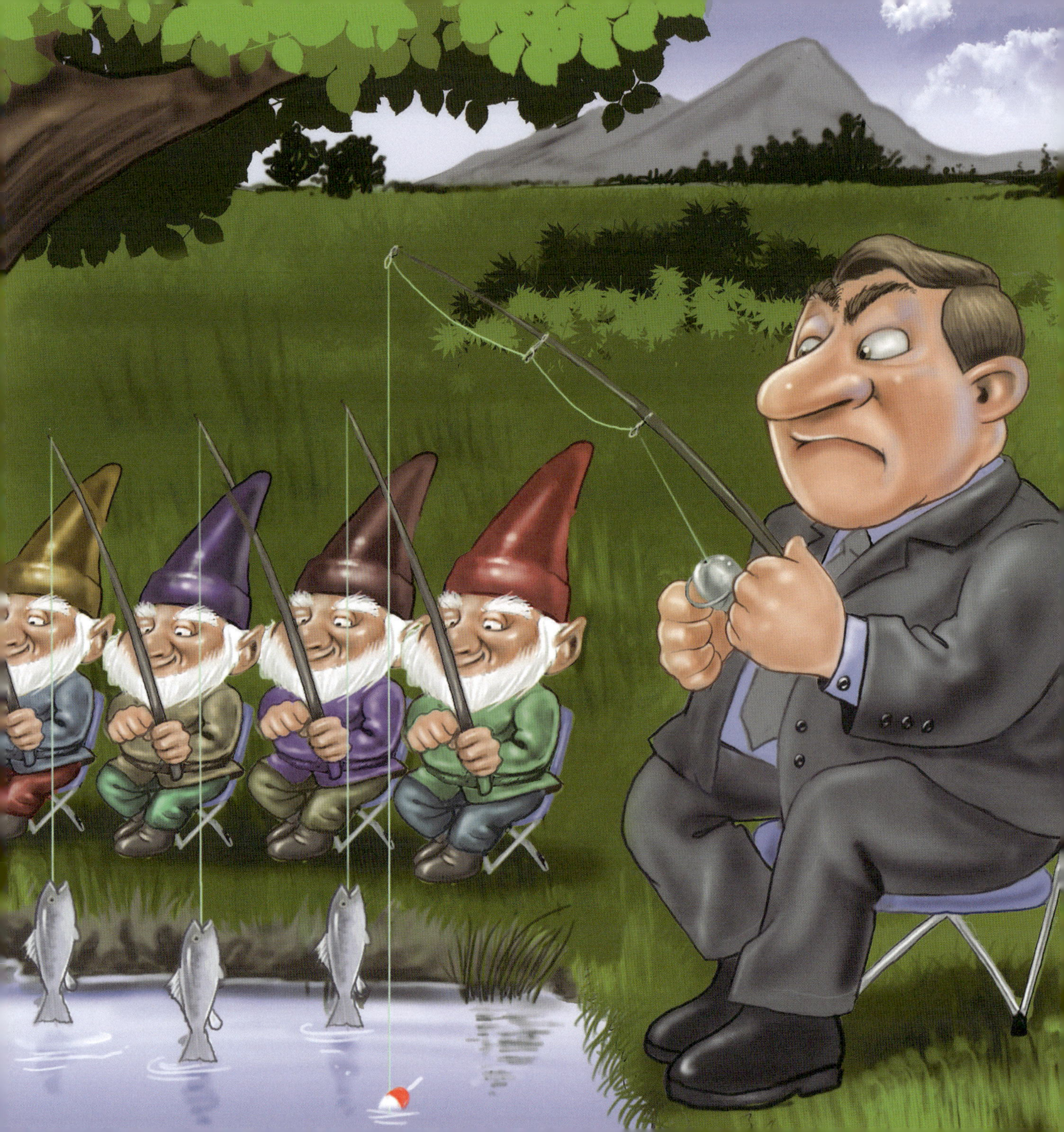

Buzzwords & BS | Stephen Kirlew

"FISH OR CUT BAIT"

The Origin
This phrase originated in the 19th century referring to fishermen divvying up the day's tasks - who would cut bait and who would fish. As phrases go, this fishy one's certainly 'catchy'. Get it?!

The Meaning
This aquatic phrase is used in a business setting to indicate that it's time to make a decision and/or take action, or withdraw from a task/project altogether.

Bob Sheldon says...

"It's time to fish or cut bait on this one, Mark. Are you having tuna or chicken at tomorrow's business lunch?"

Employee of the Month
January
February
March
April
August
October
November
December

Buzzwords & BS | Stephen Kirlew

"FLAVOR OF THE MONTH"

The Origin

This phrase originated in the 1930s as a slogan devised by the Saltease ice cream company to promote their range of new flavors. Personally, my 'flavor of the month' —and the year— is peanut butter swirl.

The Meaning

In corporate speak, the 'flavor of the month' is the newest fad, or CEO's favorite person, that is popular for a moment in time. But be warned: it's often for a short period of time.

Bob Sheldon says...

" Let's face it, Louise, you're just not 'flavor of the month'. Or next month. Or the following month. Or the one after that! "

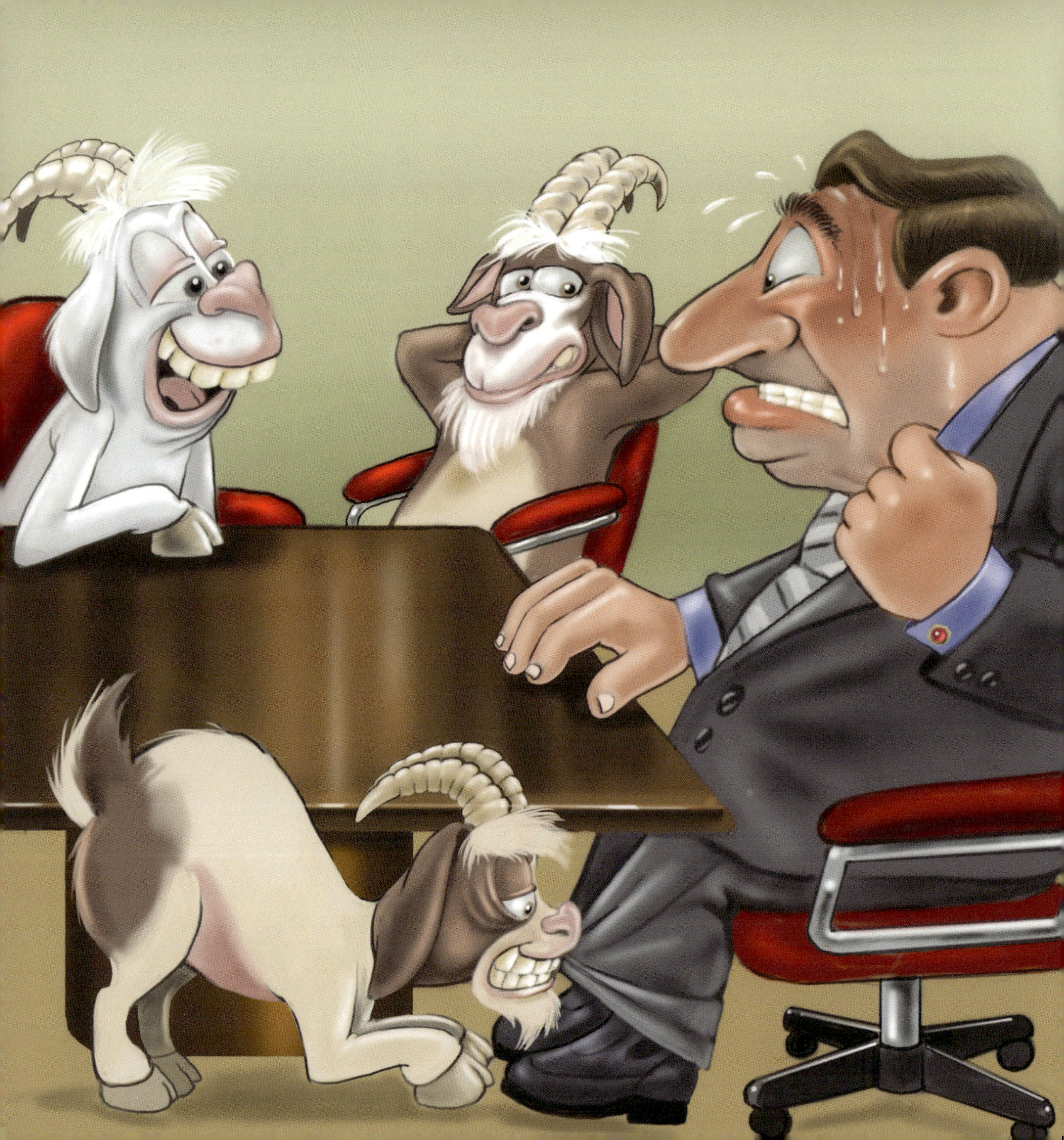

Buzzwords & BS | Stephen Kirlew

"GOAT RODEO"

The Origin
It's believed this term is linked to a family of goat-related terms with one thing in common - they relate to chaotic situations. Did you know goats have four stomachs? I'm not kidding. Get it? Kid-ding!

The Meaning
This business buzzword is used to describe a meeting or event that is particularly chaotic and impossible to manage.

Bob Sheldon says...

> "Trying to control that meeting was like being in charge of a goat rodeo. And I'm allergic to goats."

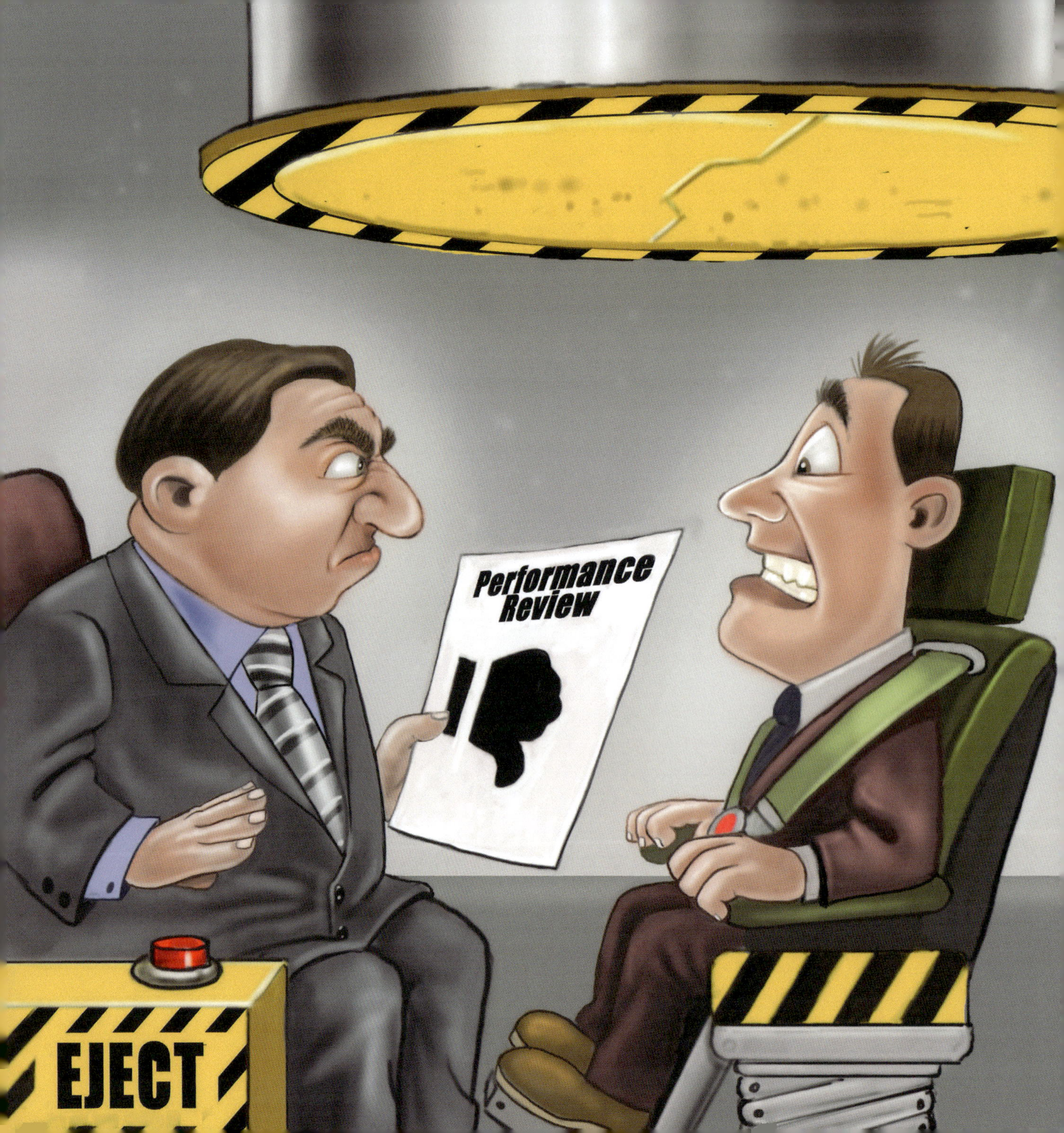
Performance
Review
EJECT

Buzzwords & BS | Stephen Kirlew

"GOING FORWARD"

The Origin
Looking backward at the origins of 'going forward' isn't easy – it seems to have always existed - but you're in fantastic company if you use this mildly-threatening buzzword. I use it almost daily.

The Meaning
On the face of it this phrase suggests 'from now on' and 'in the future,' but, in a business setting, beware a passive aggressive undertone – e.g. to lay down the law and tell everyone in no uncertain terms this is how things will be done from now on.

Bob Sheldon says...

> "Based on your performance review, Ryan, I'm giving you a new role on this project. Going forward, don't get involved."

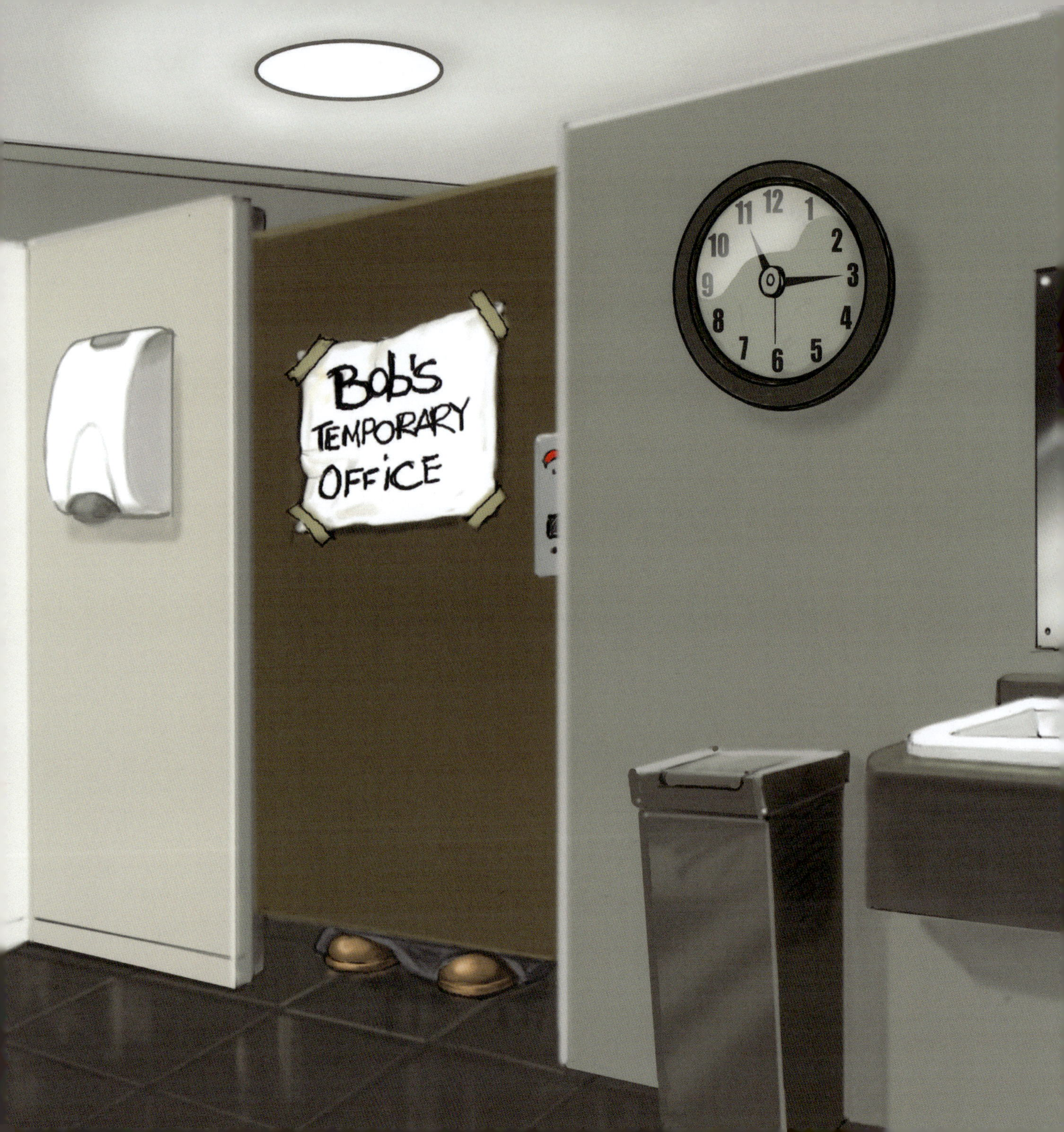
Bob's
TEMPORARY
OFFICE

Buzzwords & BS | Stephen Kirlew

"HARD STOP"

The Origin
After discovering that this phrase also refers to a mechanical device that limits the travel of a mechanism, my research into the origin of 'hard stop' came to a... hard stop.

The Meaning
A 'hard stop' is a non-negotiable cut-off time, often announced at the start of a meeting to let the attendees know that it must end at that time.

Bob Sheldon says...

"I have a hard stop at 11:15am. It's also known as a restroom break. I'm very regular, you see. High fiber diet."

FOOD

Buzzwords & BS | Stephen Kirlew

"HELICOPTER VIEW"

The Origin
This buzzword refers to the actual views from helicopters featured on TV News. The most famous example is OJ Simpson's slow-speed white Bronco chase back in 1994 which drew a huge TV audience and saw Dominos report record sales of pizza.

The Meaning
If a '30,000 foot view' is too vague, try a 'helicopter view'. It's still a high-level overview of the big picture, but with more detail. This buzzword is often used interchangeably with '30,000 foot view'.

Bob Sheldon says:...

> "You want a helicopter view of your career prospects, Tim? Buckle up, there's turbulence ahead."

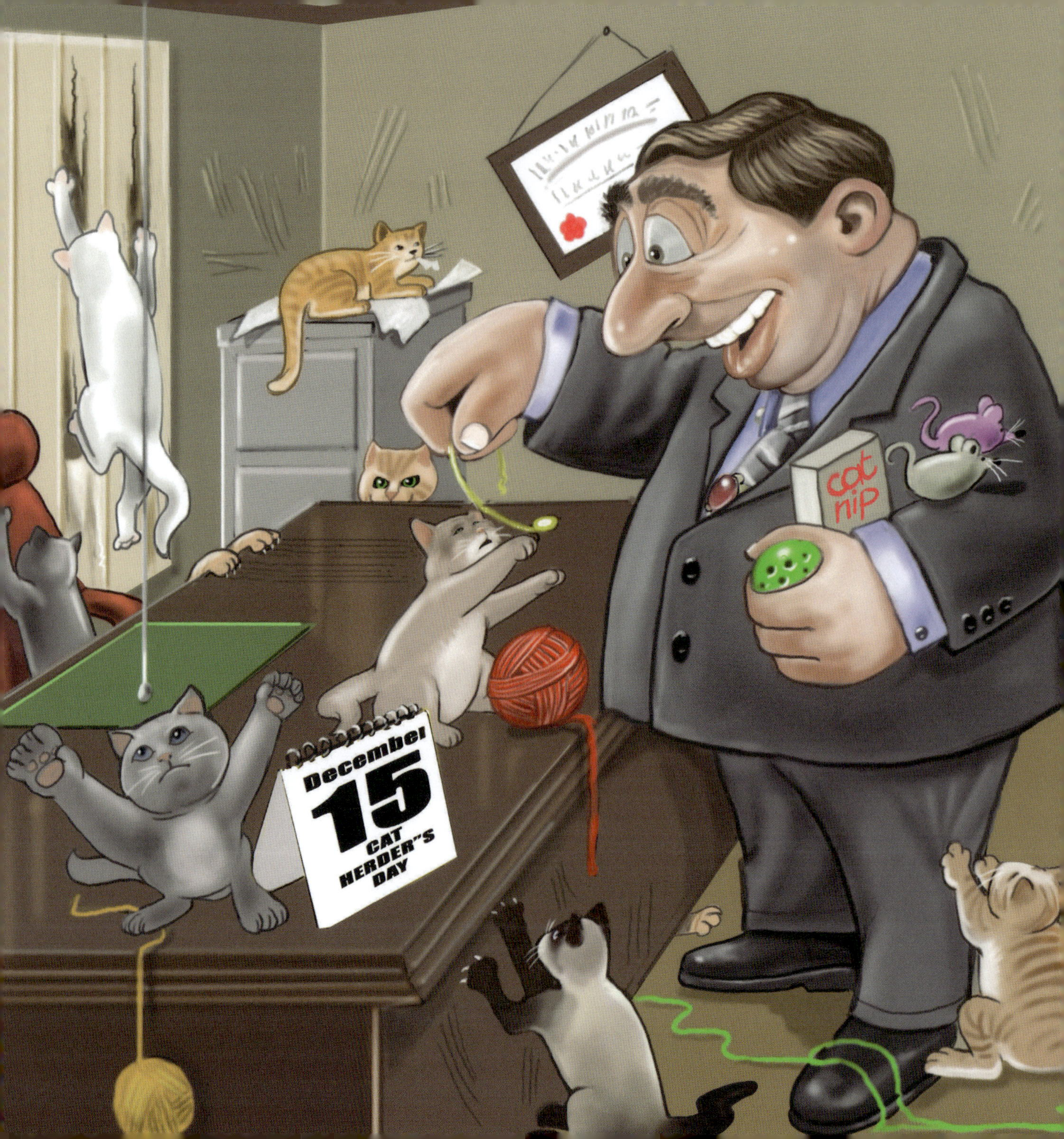
cat nip
December
15
CAT HERDER'S DAY

Buzzwords & BS | Stephen Kirlew

"HERDING CATS"

The Origin

One of the most famous early references to herding cats is in the opening scene of Monty Python's Life of Brian (1979). There's even an official Cat Herders Day on December 15th.

Purr-t the date on your calendar!

The Meaning

'Herding cats' is used to describe the futile attempt to organize a team/department who are inherently uncontrollable – cats have their own minds after all.

Bob Sheldon says...

> "Managing this department is like herding cats... I have to bribe them with edible treats!"

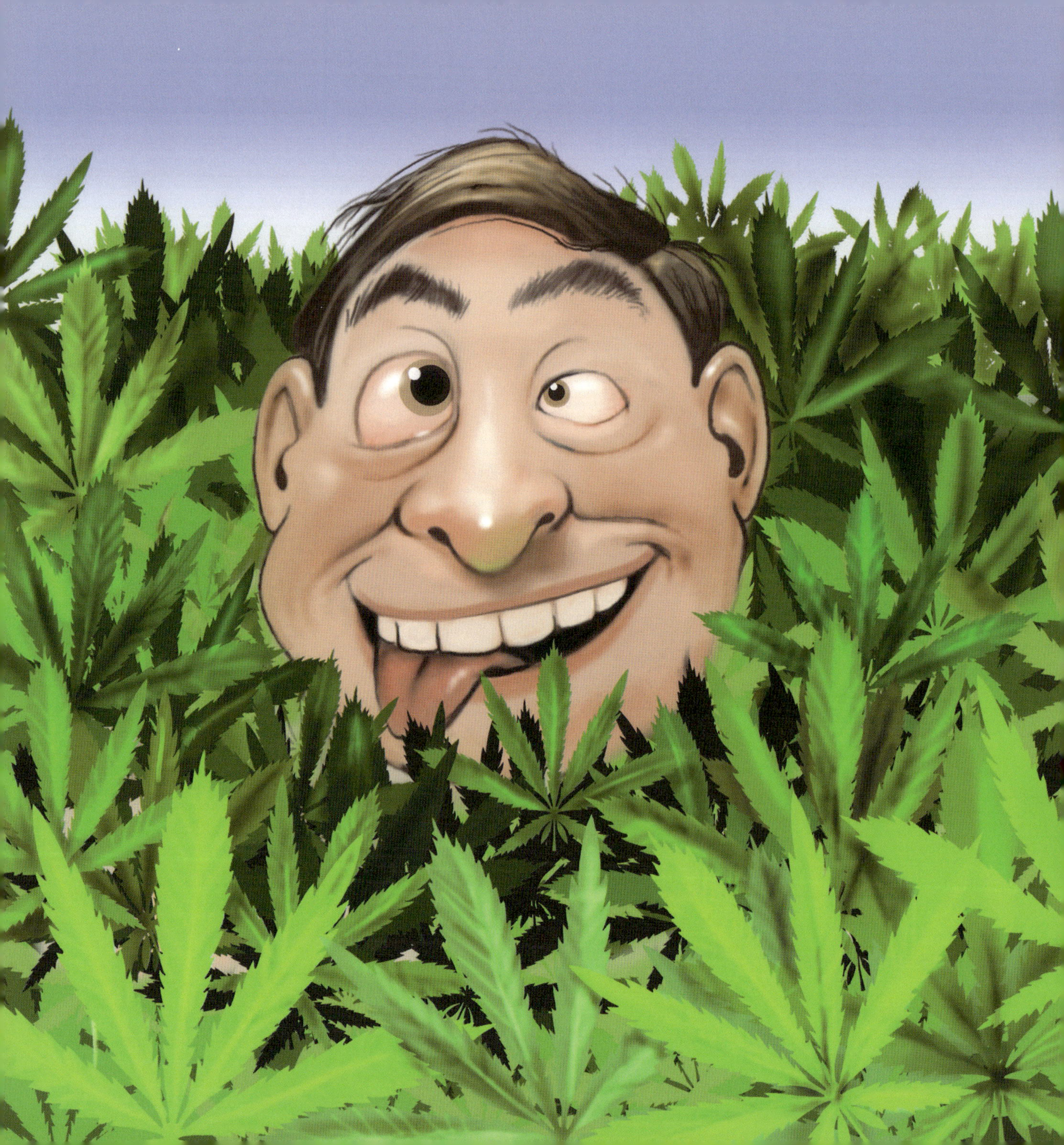

Buzzwords & BS | Stephen Kirlew

"IN THE WEEDS"

The Origin

This buzzword describes a golf ball landing in the rough making it hard for play to continue. Speaking of golf, Mark Twain described it as a 'good walk spoiled'. I wouldn't know about that--I always drive a golf cart.

The Meaning

In a business context, getting 'in the weeds' means delving deep into the details. It can highlight feeling lost in information, losing control, and not getting closer to a solution. This buzzword is the opposite of a 30,000 foot view or helicopter view.

Bob Sheldon says...

"Someone once accused me of being in the weeds. Ha! I don't go anywhere near the weeds — that's what Mr. Hannon is for."

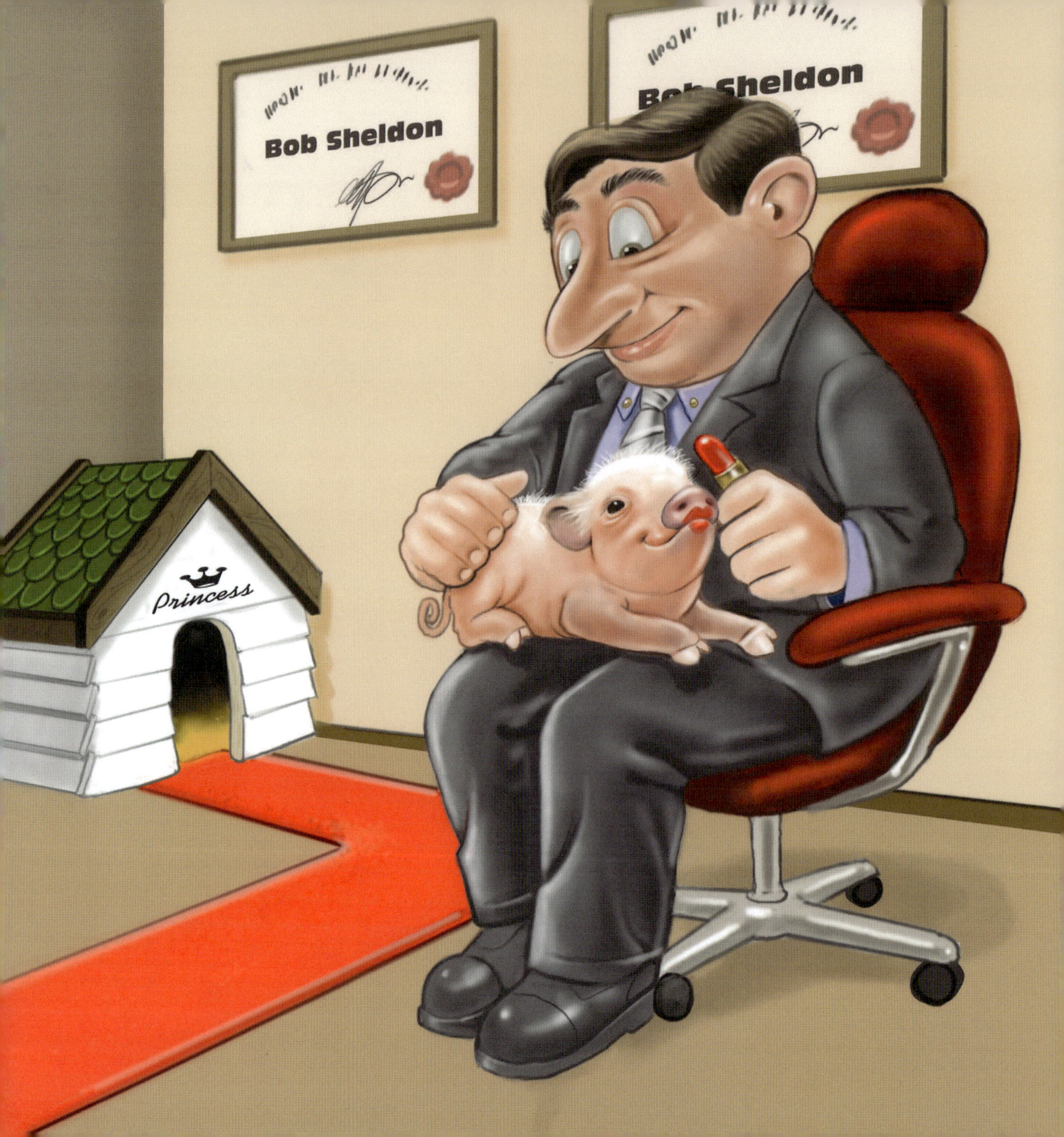
Bob Sheldon
Princess

Buzzwords & BS | Stephen Kirlew

"LIPSTICK ON A PIG"

The Origin

Variations of this porcine phrase, such as a 1732 reference to 'A hog in armor is still but a hog', have existed since the 16th century. However, this version entered the lexicon after the word 'lipstick' was introduced in 1880.

The Meaning

To put 'lipstick on a pig' is to try and make something unpleasant seem more attractive. Barack Obama controversially used it in 2008 in reference to the Republican party's proposed policy changes.

Bob Sheldon says...

"This report is simply putting lipstick on a pig, Seth... it stinks! Maybe you should add perfume?"

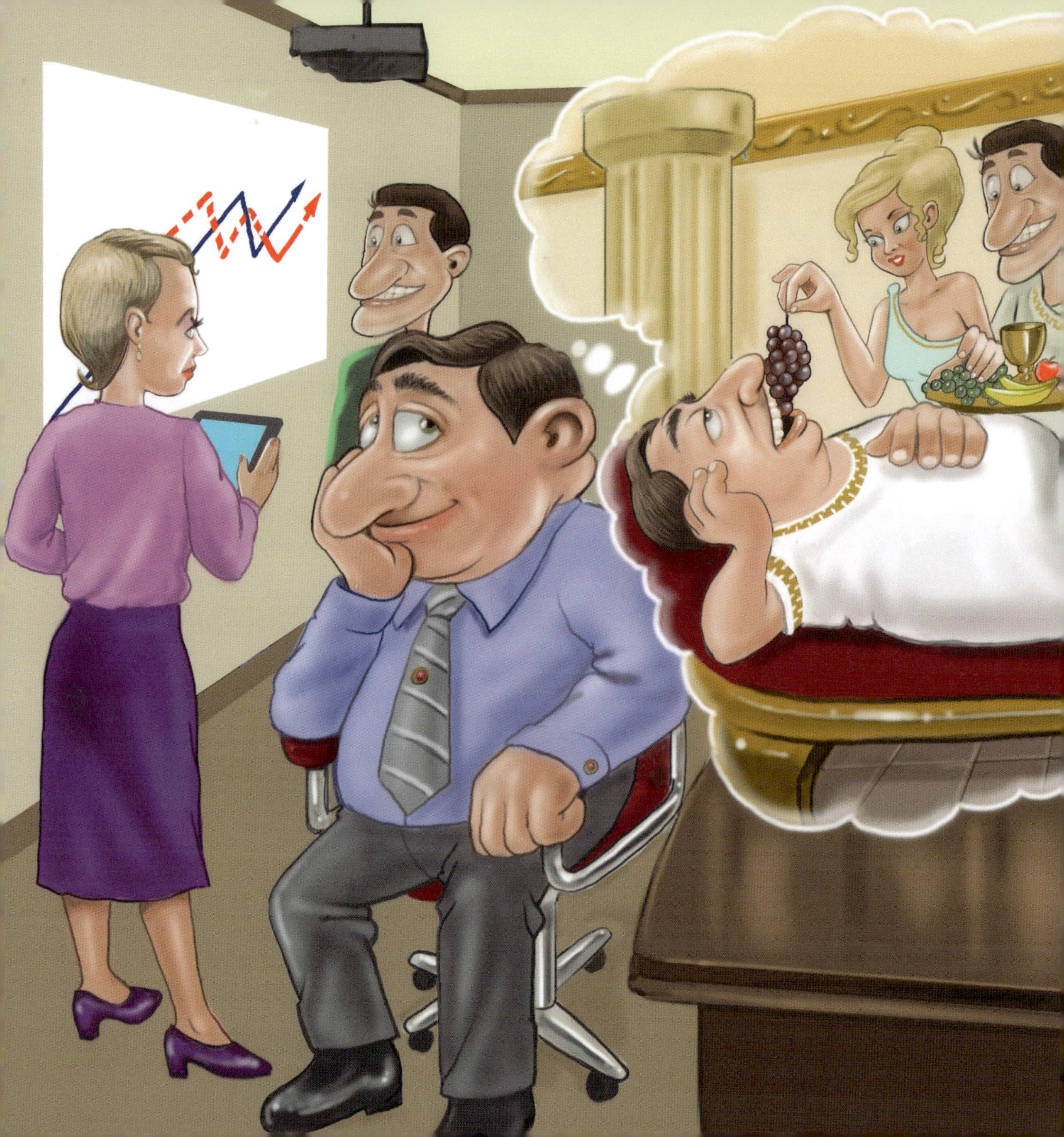

Buzzwords & BS | Stephen Kirlew

"LOW-HANGING FRUIT"

The Origin
Similar fruity phrases have been used since the 17th century. Another famous piece of low-hanging fruit from the 17th century is Sir Isaac Newton's apple. He's lucky it wasn't a falling coconut. It's estimated they kill 150 people a year.

The Meaning
When picking fruit, it's easier to pick from the lower branches. In business terms, the 'low-hanging fruit' refers to the easy targets and quick wins one can take to achieve success.

Bob Sheldon says...

> "My doctor said I should eat better. I told her I always reach for low-hanging fruit!"

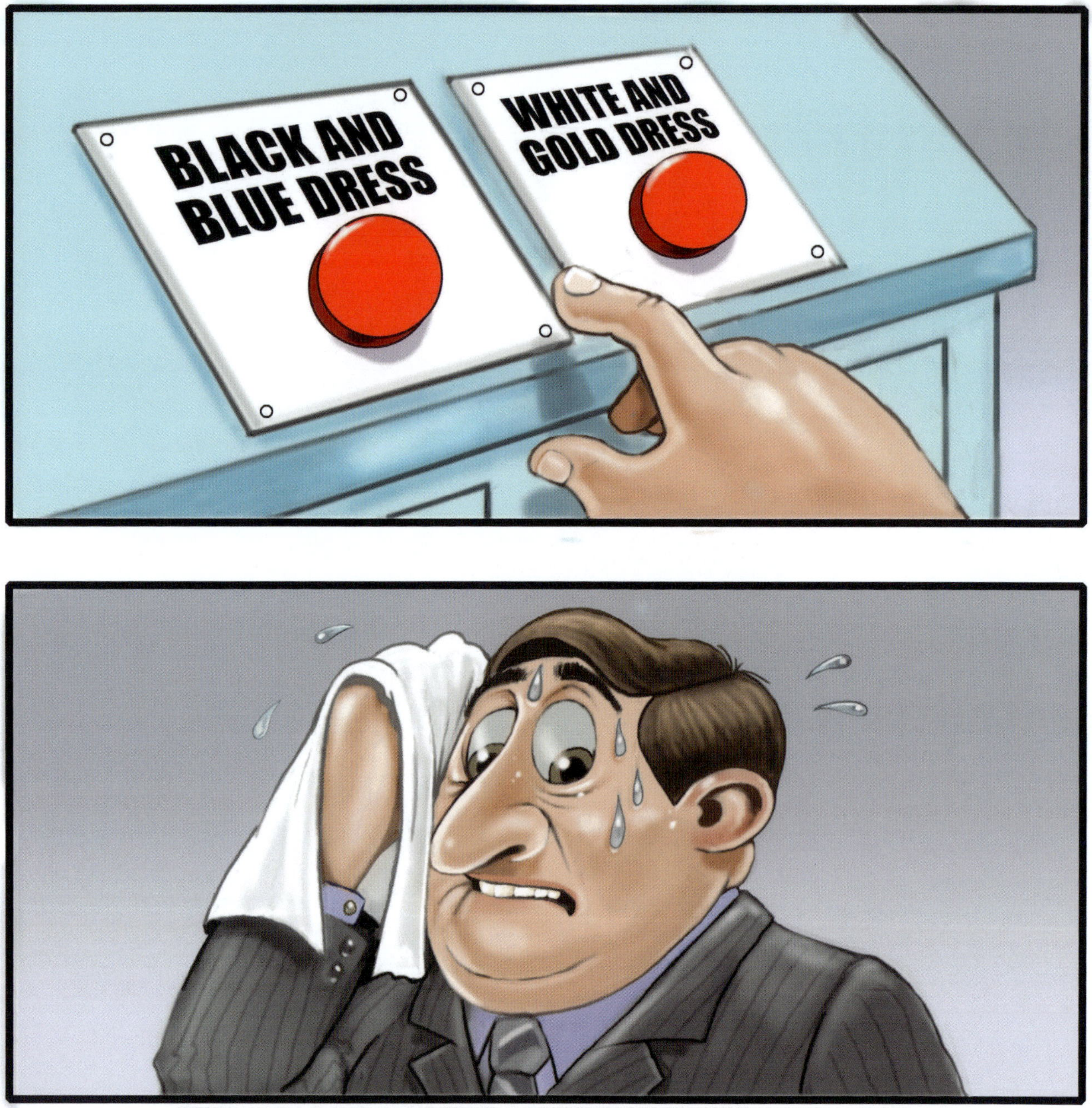
BLACK AND BLUE DRESS
WHITE AND GOLD DRESS

Buzzwords & BS | Stephen Kirlew

"MISSION-CRITICAL"

The Origin

It's likely that the phrase originally referred to the importance of navigational systems in air and space travel. The term later entered the business lexicon in tandem with the rise of the internet as an essential business system.

The Meaning

If something is 'mission-critical' to a business it means that should it fail or get disrupted it would cause the firm to cease operating successfully.

Bob Sheldon says...

"Getting you to hit this month's sales target isn't mission critical, Steve. It's Mission Impossible."

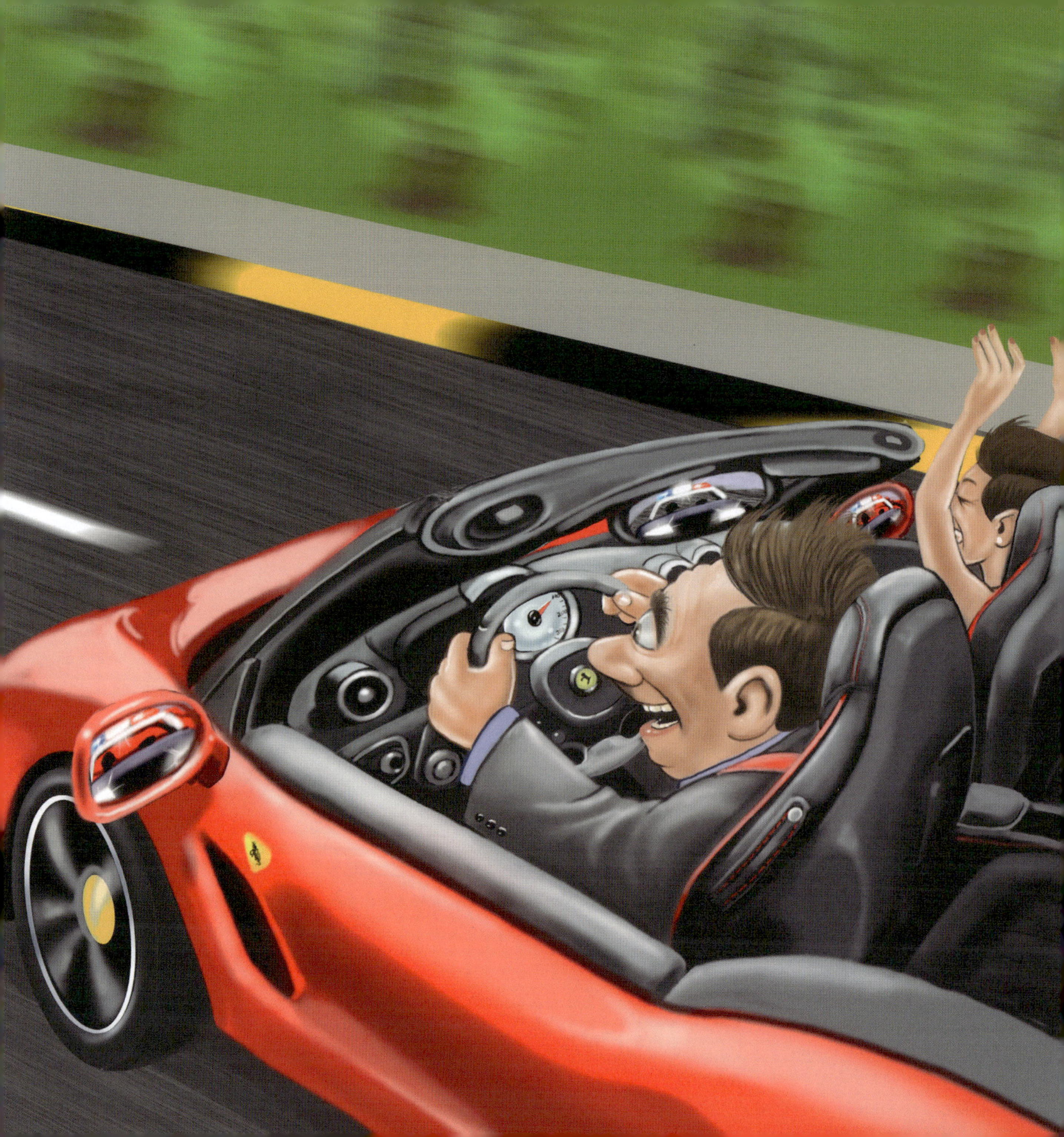

Buzzwords & BS | Stephen Kirlew

"MOVE THE NEEDLE"

The Origin

This buzzword refers to old analog meters, such as a speedometer or VU meter, which had a needle that pointed to the current value. For example, the faster I'm driving my imaginary Lamborghini Urus, the further the needle will move along the scale.

The Meaning

To 'move the needle' is to cause a noticeable reaction, hopefully positive, to a situation. Usually referring to sales figures.

Bob Sheldon says…

"We need to move the needle on the quality of balloons for the office party. But don't pop them though."

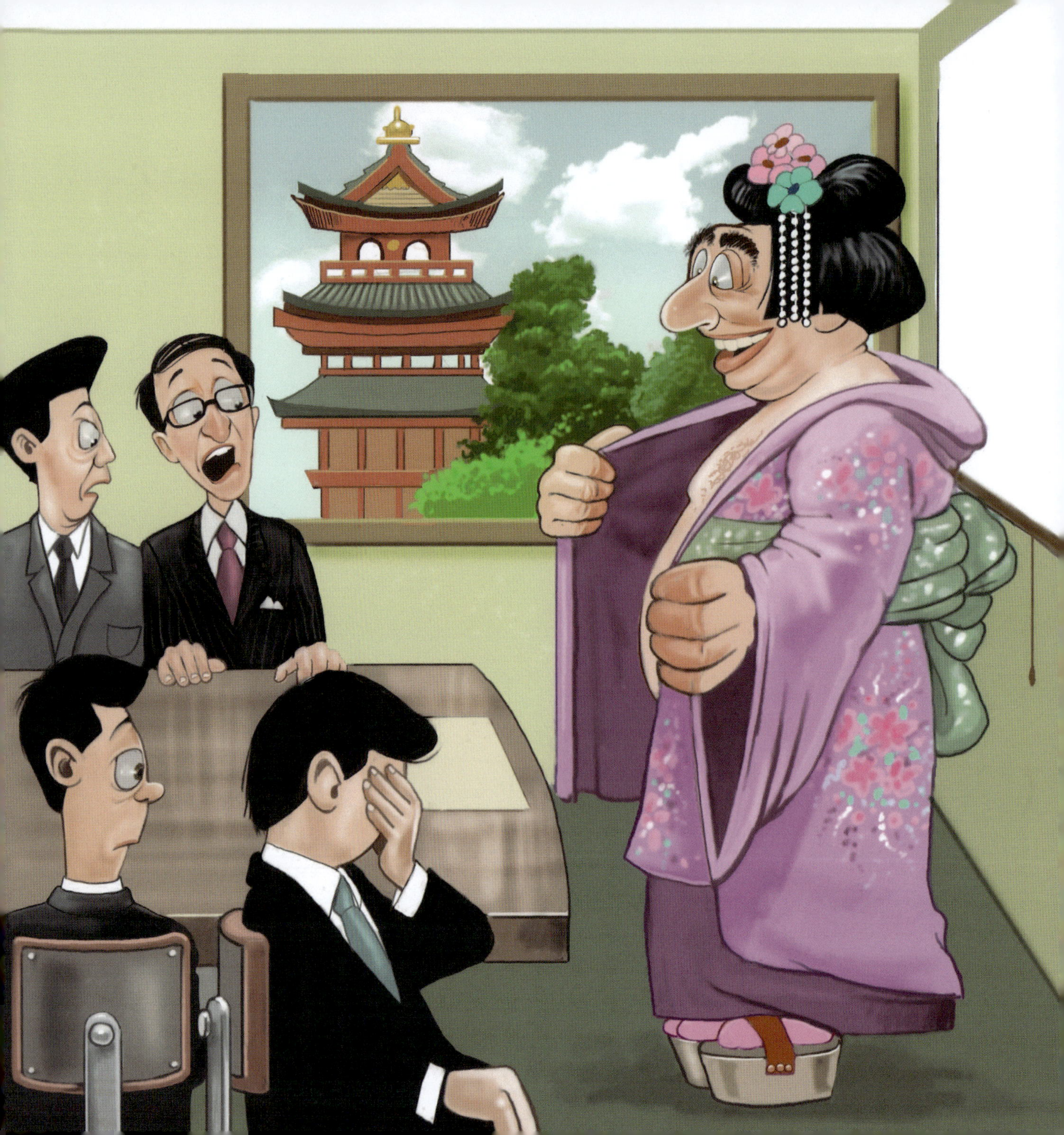

Buzzwords & BS | Stephen Kirlew

"OPEN THE KIMONO"

The Origin

This somewhat politically incorrect buzzword dates back to the 1980s when there was a spate of Japanese acquisitions of American companies.

The Meaning

A kimono is a traditional Japanese garment. Opening it reveals what you're wearing (or not) underneath.

In a business context, to 'open the kimono' is to freely reveal confidential information about a deal or company.

Bob Sheldon says...

"Let's open the kimono, Mr. Yakomoto. If I like what I see, we're having sushi to celebrate."

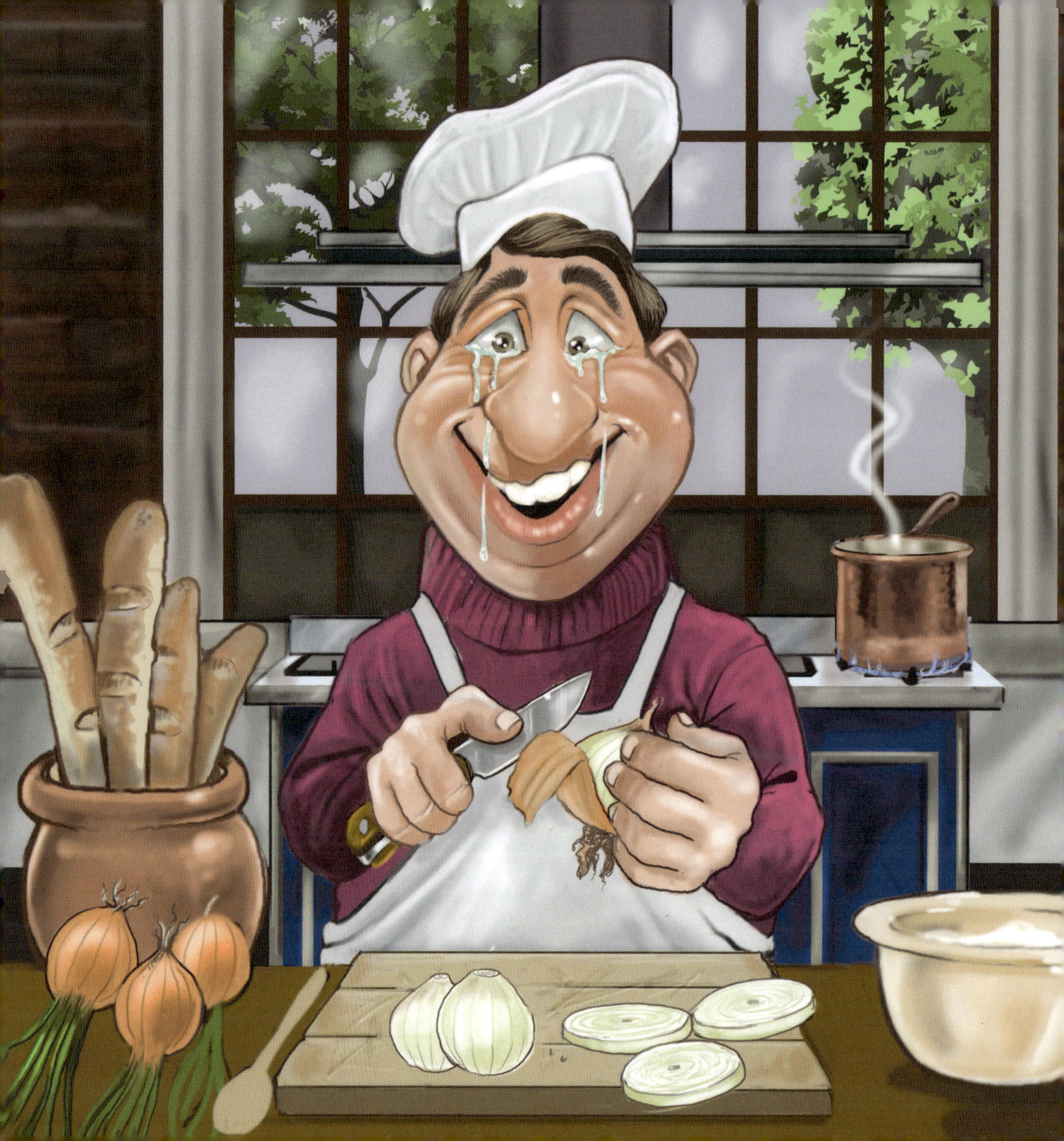

Buzzwords & BS | Stephen Kirlew

"PEEL BACK THE ONION"

The Origin
Comparisons between onions and other objects with multiple layers have been made forever and a day. There was even a mention in the 2001 movie Shrek: "Onions have layers. Ogres have layers".

The Meaning
This dramatic way of saying 'let's take a closer look at the problem one step at a time' is so overused in some boardrooms, it brings a tear to one's eyes.

Bob Sheldon says...

> "I'm a master of peeling back the onion, Holly, because I have one thing in common with onions... We both make grown men cry."

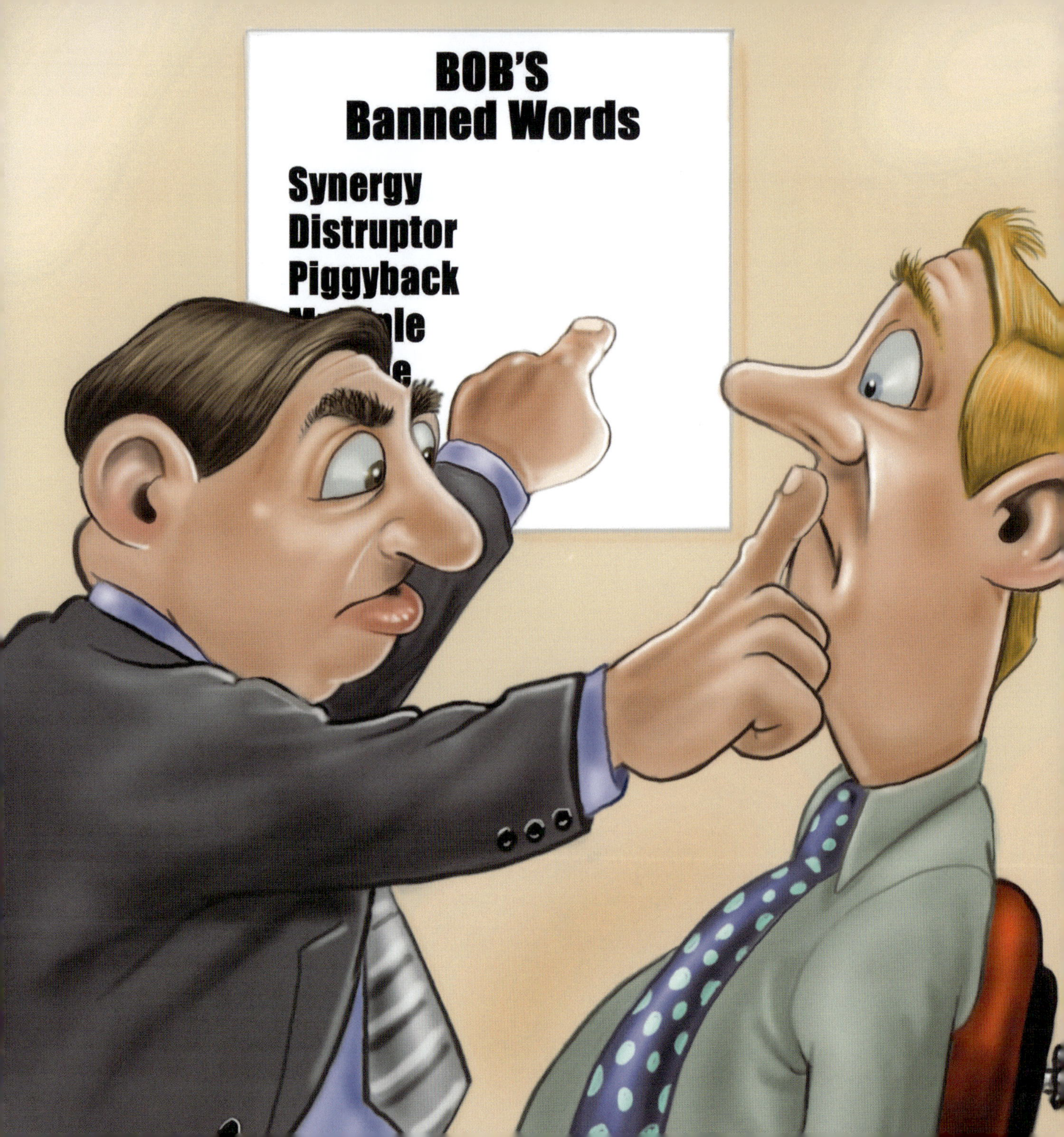
BOB'S
Banned Words
Synergy
Distruptor
Piggyback

"PIGGYBACK"

The Origin

In the 16th century, pick pack meant to carry someone on your back or shoulders. Over time, 'pick' became 'pig' before morphing into 'piggyback'. No pigs were harmed in the naming of this buzzword.

The Meaning

This, the second pig-related buzzword in this book, means to build upon (or repeat with slightly different wording) someone else's idea or comment to try and take it one step further.

Bob Sheldon says...

"I've banned the word 'piggyback' in the office. With three kids and two grandkids, just hearing the word makes my knees ache."

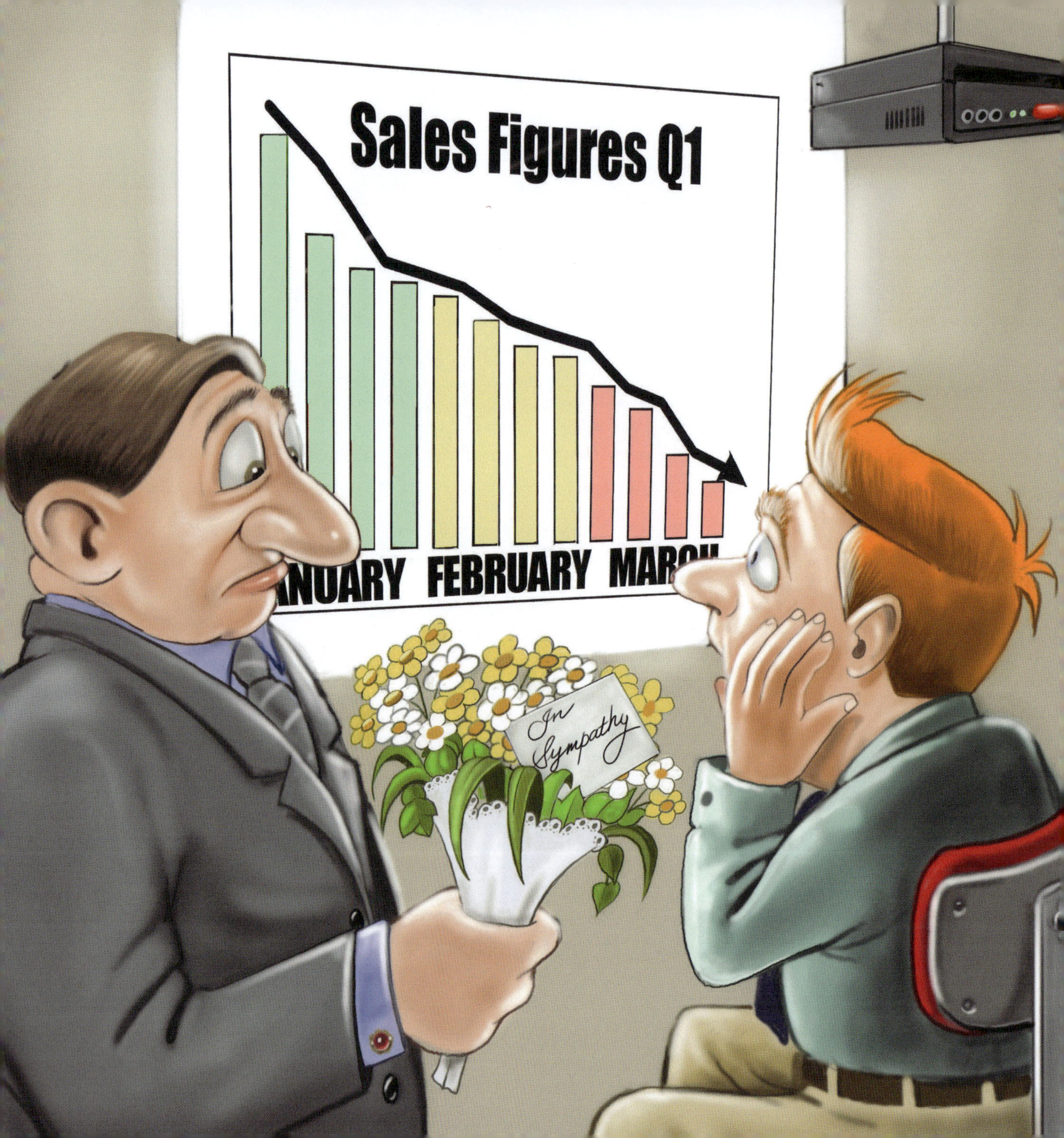
Sales Figures Q1
FEBRUARY
In Sympathy

Buzzwords & BS | Stephen Kirlew

"POST-MORTEM"

The Origin

'Post-mortem' is Latin for 'after death'. After a person dies, a post-mortem examination takes place to determine the cause and time of death.

The Meaning

This corporate cliché is used to describe an analysis or dissection of the key takeaways of a completed project, meeting, or event.

Bob Sheldon says...

"You want an honest post-mortem on that meeting, Wes? It was DOA."

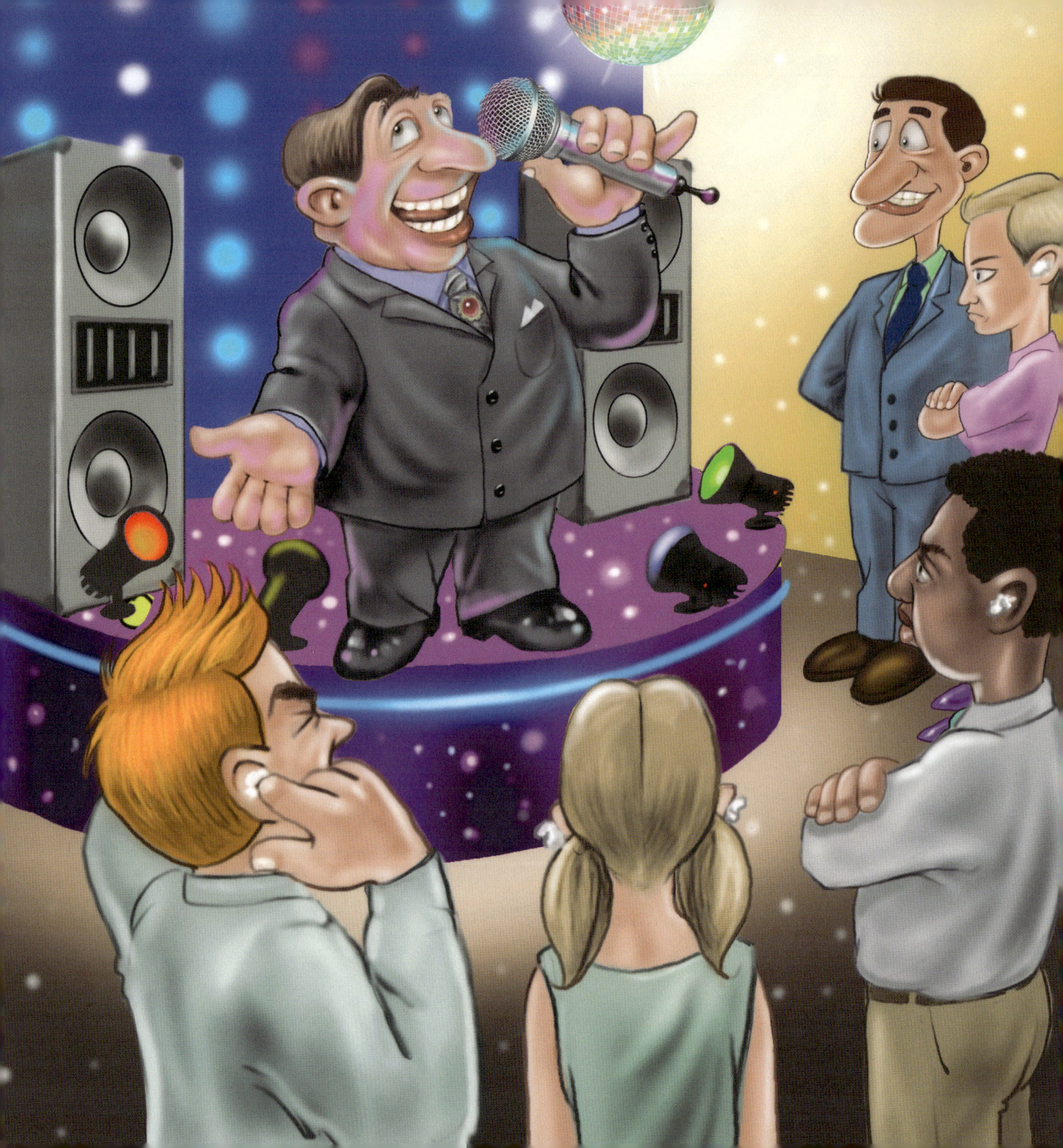

Buzzwords & BS | Stephen Kirlew

"PULSE CHECK"

The Origin

The pulse check - introduced by Italian physician Santorio Santorio in the 17th century to measure how fast someone's heart was beating - is a common practice today. He also checked his metabolism by weighing his excrement - a not so common practice today.

The Meaning

In a business setting, a pulse check is a short meeting or chat to check the status of an ongoing project. Employee pulse checks are surveys completed to capture their thoughts on a project or business idea.

Bob Sheldon says...

"To see what song my team wanted me to sing at the office karaoke night, I did an employee pulse check. No one replied, but *I Will Survive*."

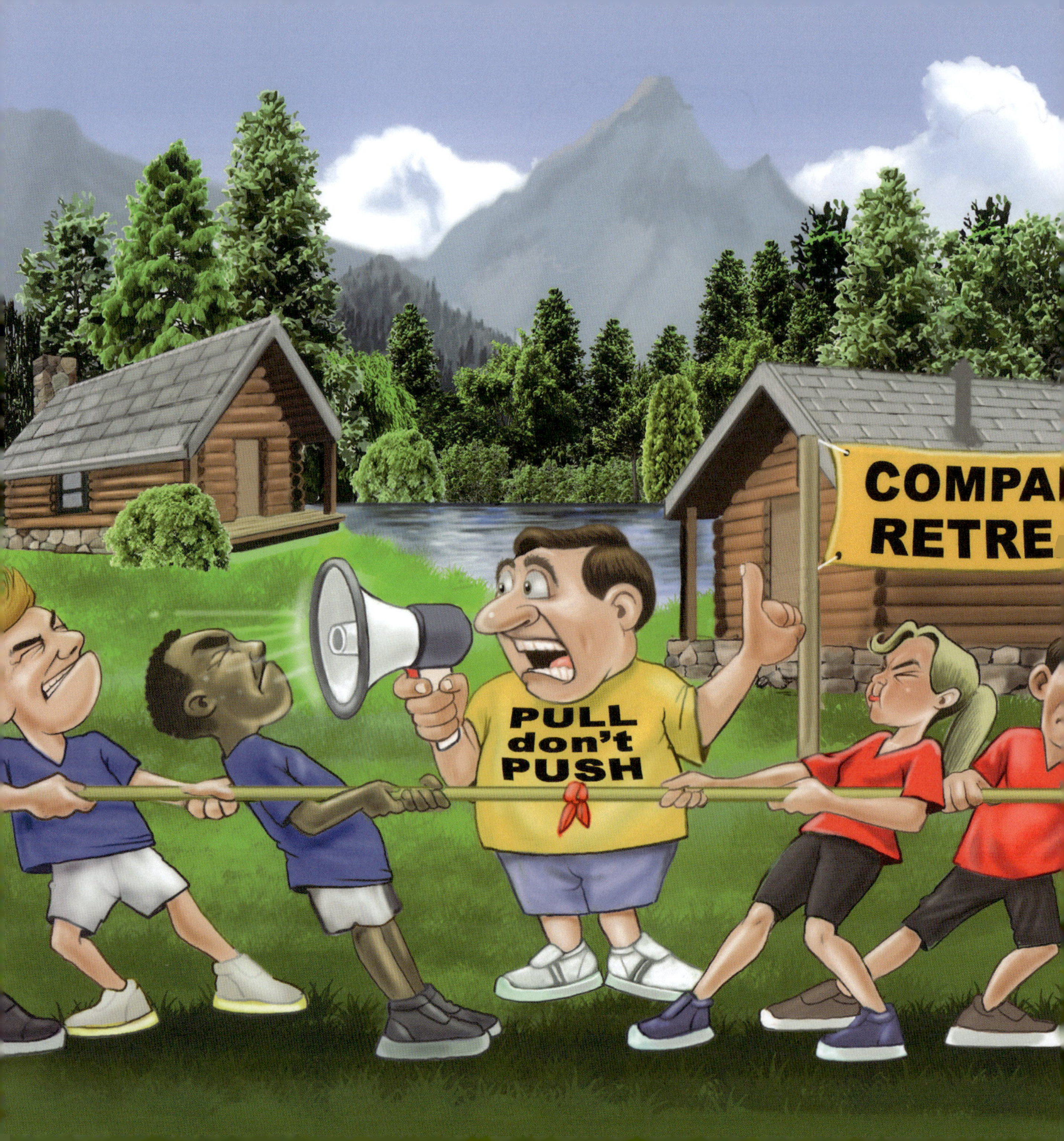
COMPA
RETRE
PULL
don't
PUSH

Buzzwords & BS | Stephen Kirlew

"PUSHING ROPE"

The Origin

The phrase 'pushing on a rope' was popularized by Congressman T. Alan Goldsborough during Congressional hearings on the Banking Act of 1935. Ah, 1935 was a great year - Elvis was born. I wonder if he used rope to walk his hound dog.

The Meaning

You can't push something with a rope, you have to pull it. To describe something as like 'pushing rope' in the business world means to undertake a futile task or to work with extremely difficult people.

Bob Sheldon says...

"I'm not pushy, I'm pull-y."

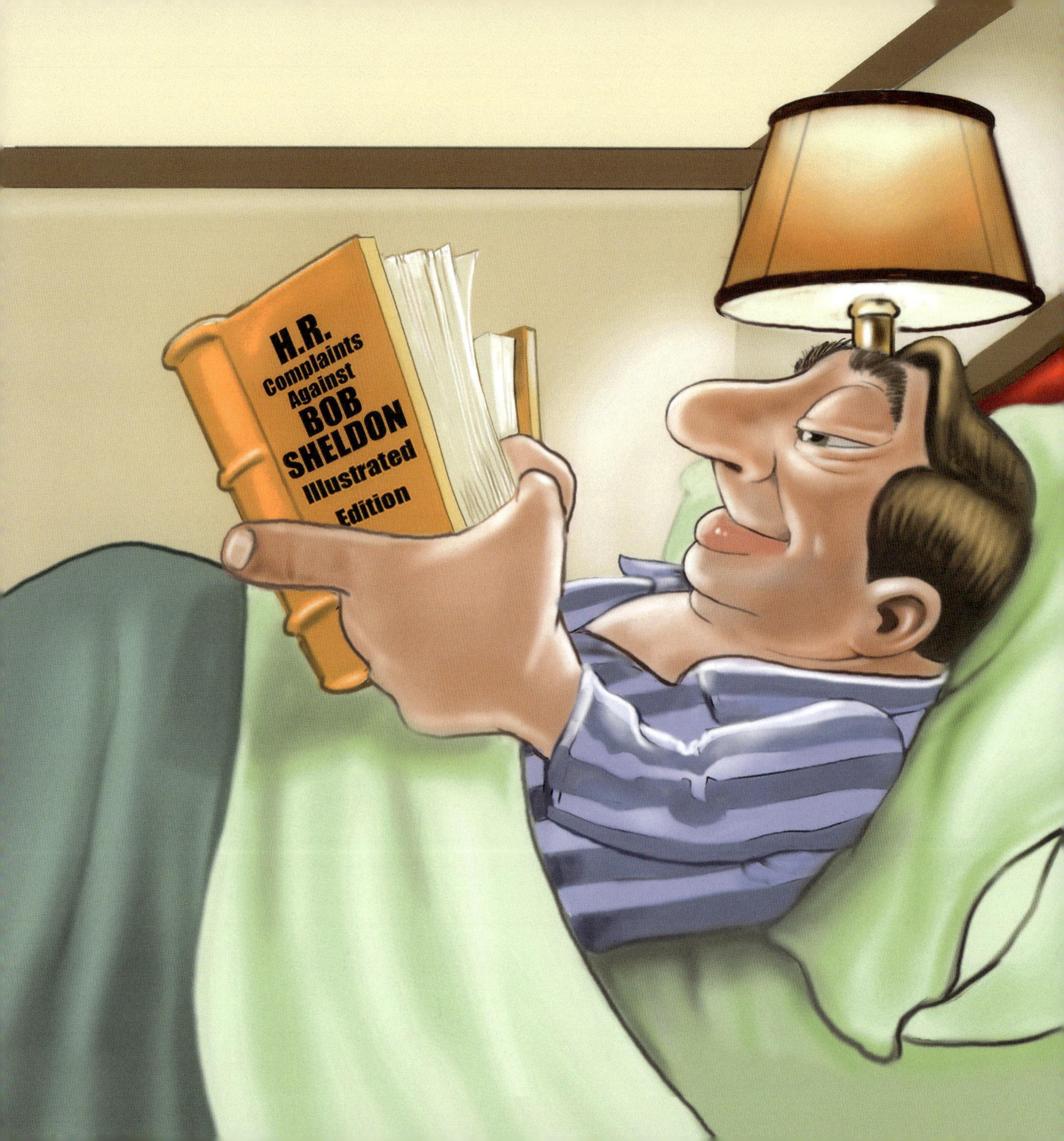
H.R.
Complaints
Against
BOB
SHELDON
Illustrated
Edition

Buzzwords & BS | Stephen Kirlew

"PUT TO BED"

The Origin
In the traditional sense, this means to literally help someone to go to bed. In the publishing world it indicates that a publication is ready to be sent to press and printed.

The Meaning
To 'put to bed' is to complete the final step in a process so you can stop working on it and move on to another project.

Bob Sheldon says...

> "I said to sleep on it, but it was your decision to put it to bed, Jacqueline. Now you've made your bed, you can lie in it. I won't lose any sleep over it."

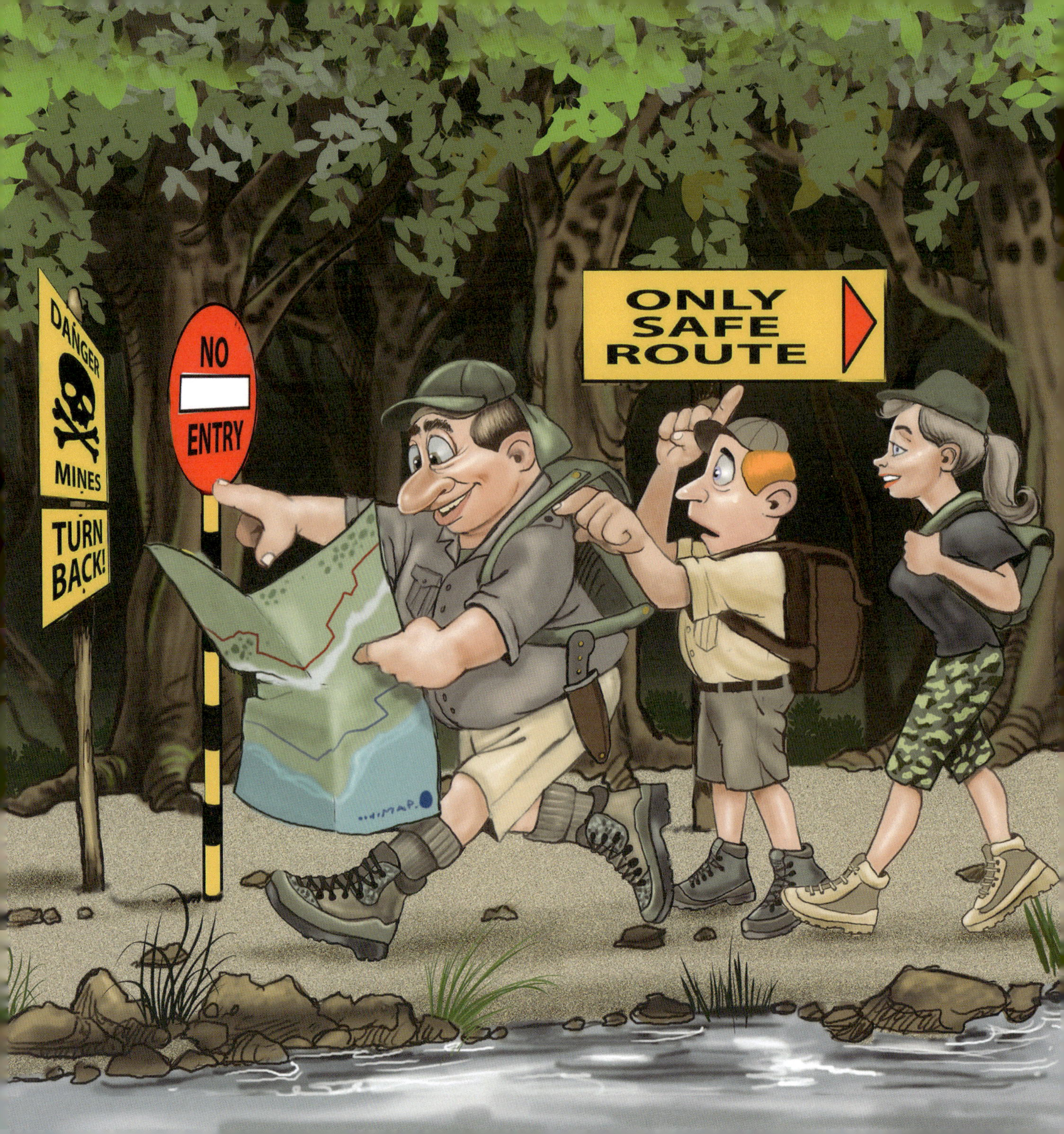
DANGER
MINES
TURN BACK!
NO
ENTRY
ONLY SAFE ROUTE
MAP

Buzzwords & BS | Stephen Kirlew

"ROADMAP"

The Origin

Roadmaps for navigational purposes date from as early as 1160 BC. One of the oldest to still exist belonged to a Roman soldier from 235 AD. I'm not sure why he needed a map though - I thought all roads lead to Rome.

The Meaning

This buzzword is used in a corporate setting to describe a detailed plan or strategy for guiding a company towards a goal.

Bob Sheldon says...

"The only way I can see Aimee successfully executing this roadmap is if she uses GPS."

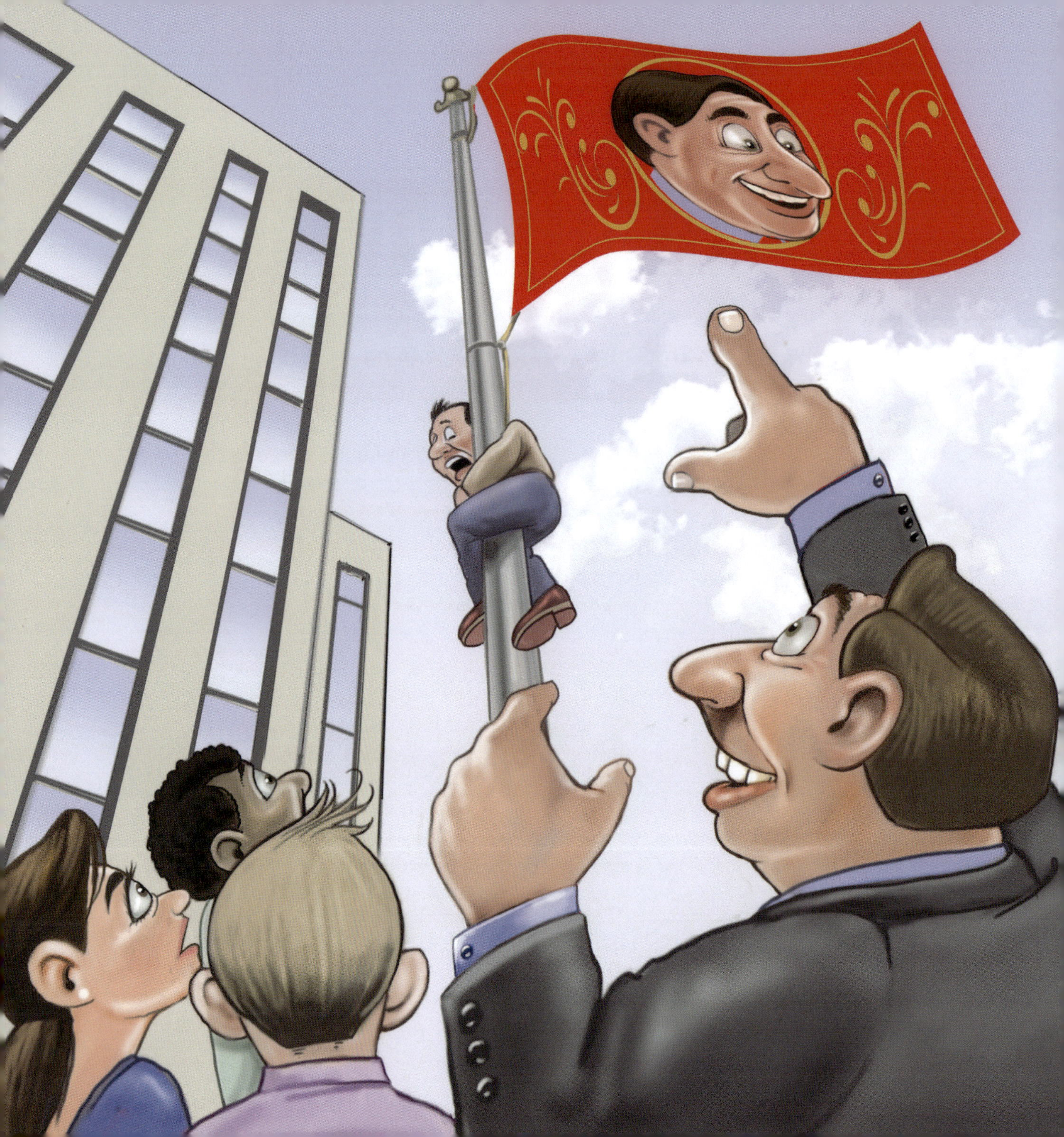

Buzzwords & BS | Stephen Kirlew

"RUN IT UP THE FLAGPOLE"

The Origin
This abbreviated version of 'let's run it up the flagpole and see if anyone salutes it' has been around since the early 1950s. As have some of my best jokes.

The Meaning
To 'run it up the flagpole' is to present a new idea to your colleagues so you can gauge their response... and hope to get a favorable one.

Bob Sheldon says...

" I'd suggest you run your idea up the flagpole before you pitch it to old man Mortimer. A very long, endless flagpole. In other words, don't pitch it to old man Mortimer. "

Bob Sheldon's
SECRET SAUCE
THE PERFECT CHOICE FOR ANY MEAL

Buzzwords & BS | Stephen Kirlew

"SECRET SAUCE"

The Origin

It wasn't just Star Wars that was all the rage in the 80s, but burger wars. As the leading burger chains went head to head to win customers, Jack in the Box marketed their mysterious 'secret sauce' to differentiate itself from other brands.

The Meaning

As a business buzzword, a company's 'secret sauce' is that all-important element that gives them a competitive advantage and increases the chances of success.

Bob Sheldon says…

"If this company were a sandwich, I'd be the secret sauce."

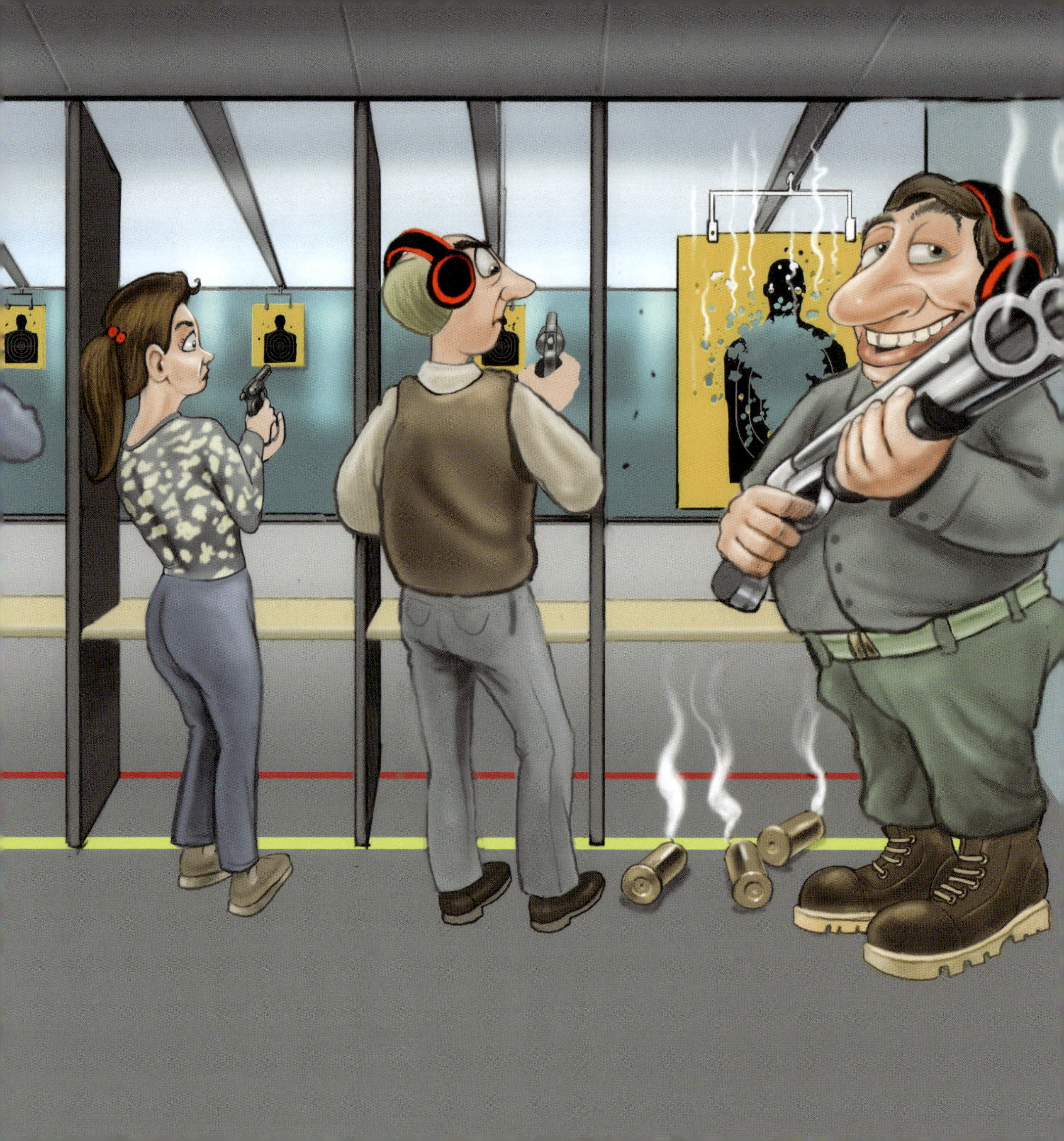

Buzzwords & BS | Stephen Kirlew

"SHOTGUN APPROACH"

The Origin
If you thought this phrase uses the analogy of a shotgun that fires a number of small pellets over a wide area, as opposed to a handgun that shoots a single bullet at a targeted area, then you're 'on target'. Get it?!

The Meaning
To use a 'shotgun approach' in a business setting is to follow a haphazard, untargeted strategy with a 'more is better' philosophy that favors quantity instead of quality.

Bob Sheldon says...

" It was brave of you to try a shotgun approach to the marketing campaign, Austin, but, unfortunately, you're firing blanks. "

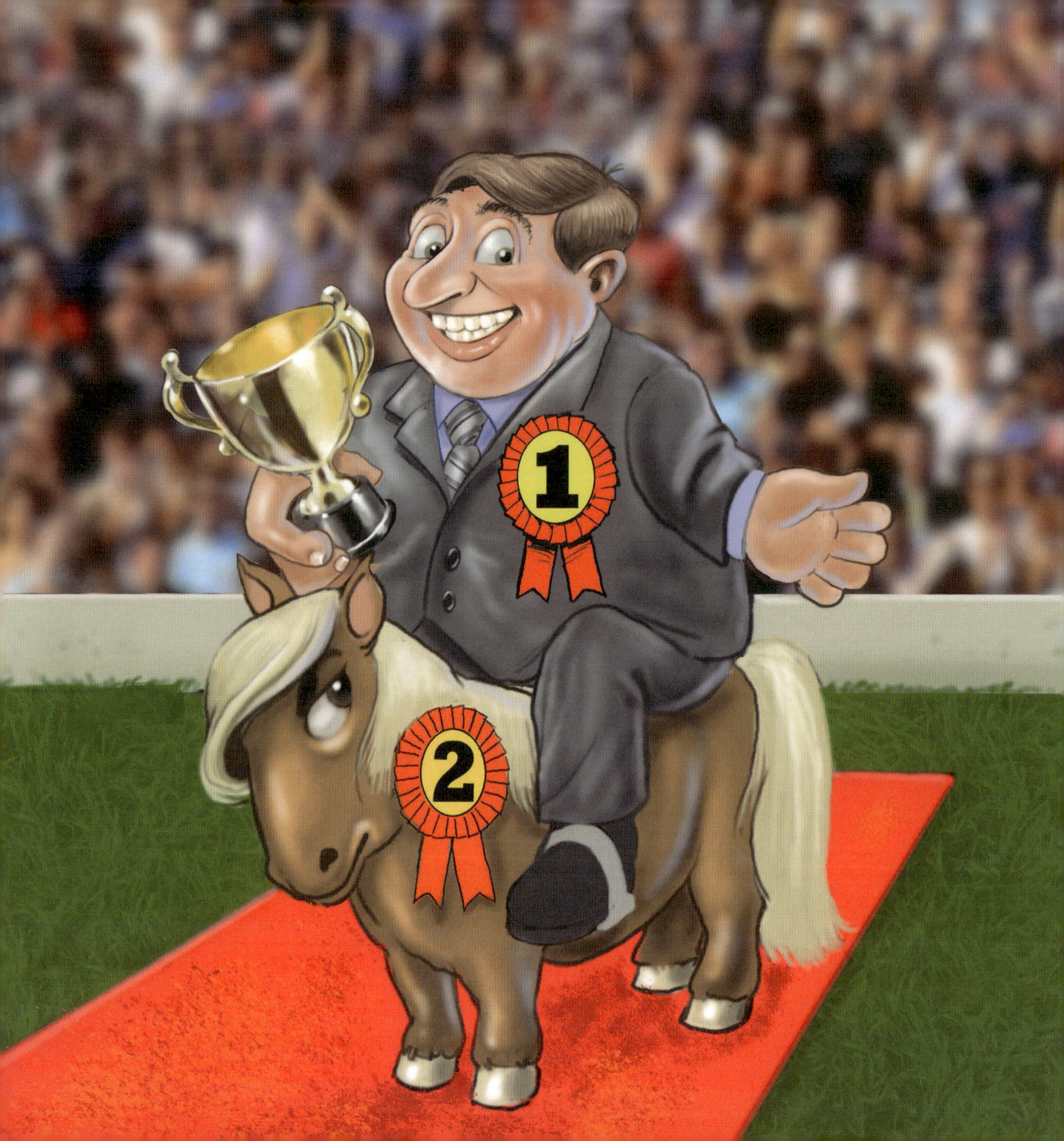
1
2

Buzzwords & BS | Stephen Kirlew

"SHOW PONY"

The Origin
Traveling circuses in the late 19th century often featured performing ponies as the main event. If they were to make a movie about it, they could call it The Greatest Showpony.

The Meaning
To describe someone as a 'show pony' means that they like to be the center of attention. While they present well, this often disguises a lack of real ability.

Bob Sheldon says...

> "You can't impress me by being the department's show pony, Andy. I'm allergic to ponies - And hard work, That's why I hired you!"

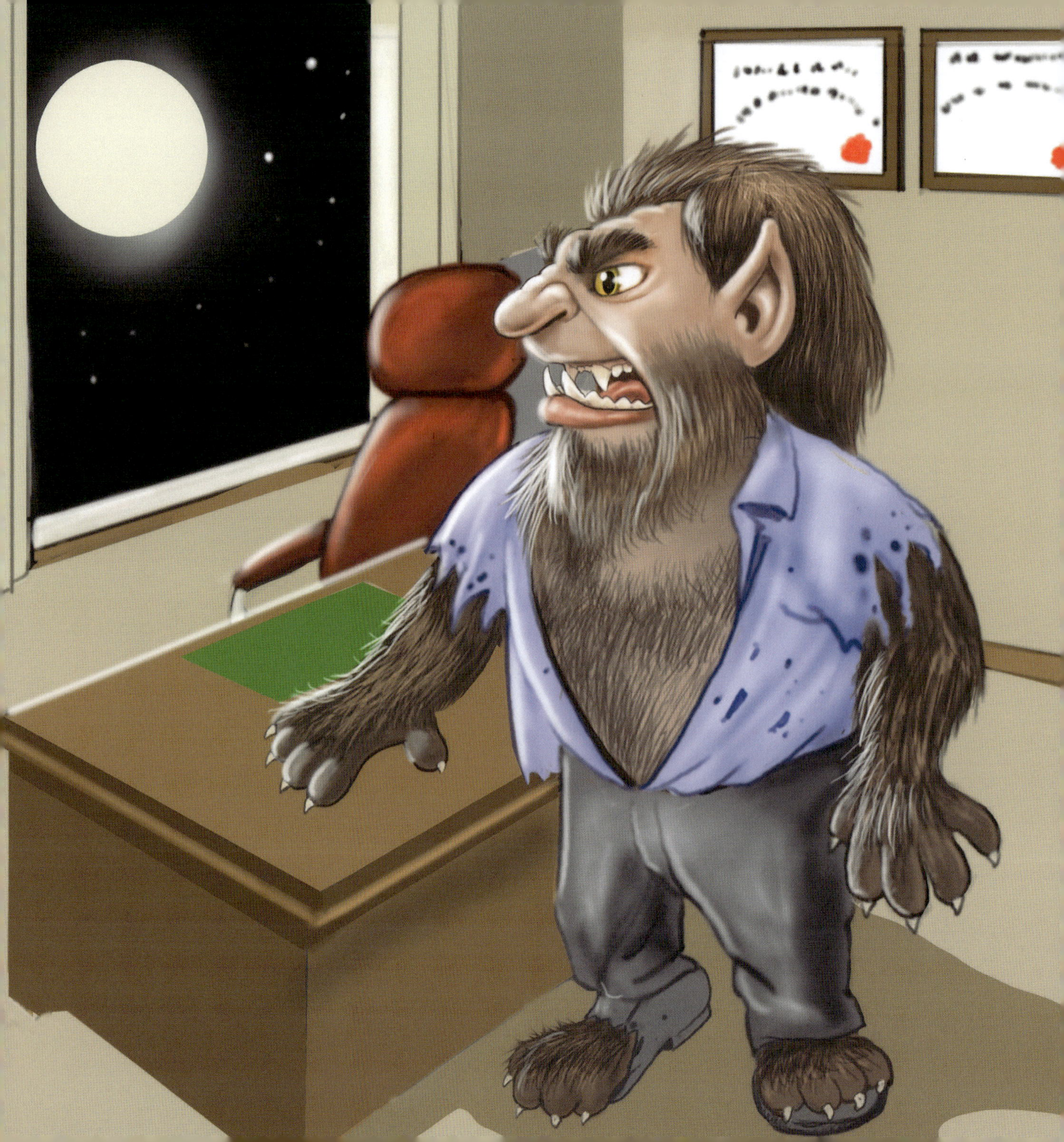

Buzzwords & BS | Stephen Kirlew

"SILVER BULLET"

The Origin

According to my grandpa, the only way to kill supernatural beings such as werewolves is to use a silver bullet. But as we all know, they don't really exist. Werewolves, that is, not grandpas.

The Meaning

As a corporate catchphrase, a 'silver bullet' is an action that provides an immediate perfect solution to a previously unsolvable problem.

Bob Sheldon says...

" There's more chance of discovering the Silver Surfer in this meeting than a silver bullet to boost these sales figures. "

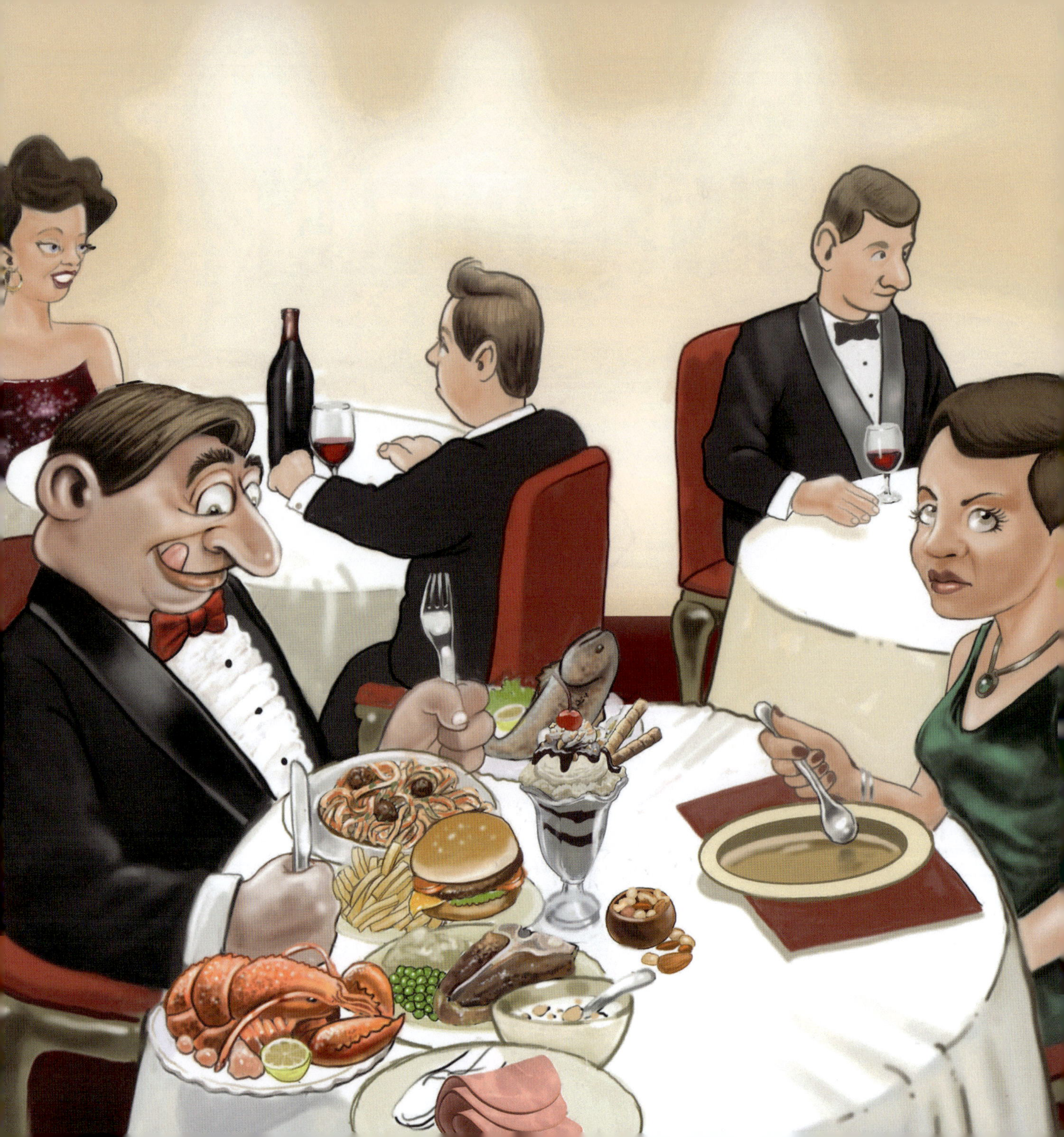

Buzzwords & BS | Stephen Kirlew

"SOUP TO NUTS"

The Origin

This phrase comes from the description of a traditional full-course dinner, from the first course of soup to a dessert of nuts and everything in between.

The Meaning

As a business buzzword, 'soup to nuts' means from start to finish or beginning to end, so a project manager may oversee every stage of a project from 'soup to nuts'.

Bob Sheldon says...

"You may have worked on the project from soup to nuts, Wendy, but I'm picking up the check."

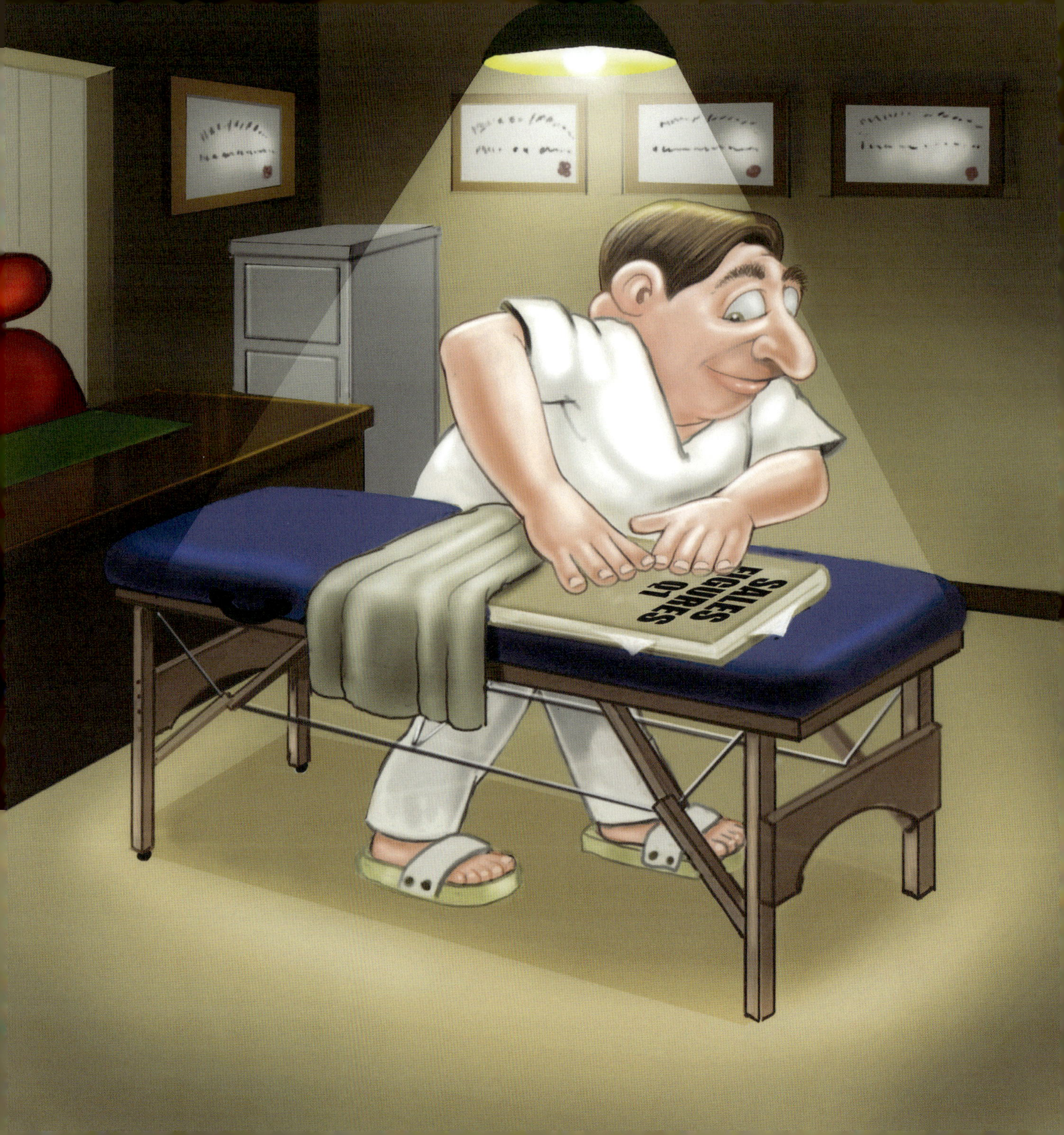
SALES
FIGURES
Q1

Buzzwords & BS | Stephen Kirlew

"STATISTICAL MASSAGE"

The Origin

The word 'massage' comes from the French for 'friction of kneading'. A recent study found that 66% of people get massages to reduce stress, and I've not massaged those figures.

The Meaning

The massaging of statistics means to present numbers in a favorable way so as to convey the desired message.

Bob Sheldon says...

"Can you give the data a statistical massage before presenting it to shareholders, Jenny? You massage my data, I'll massage yours."

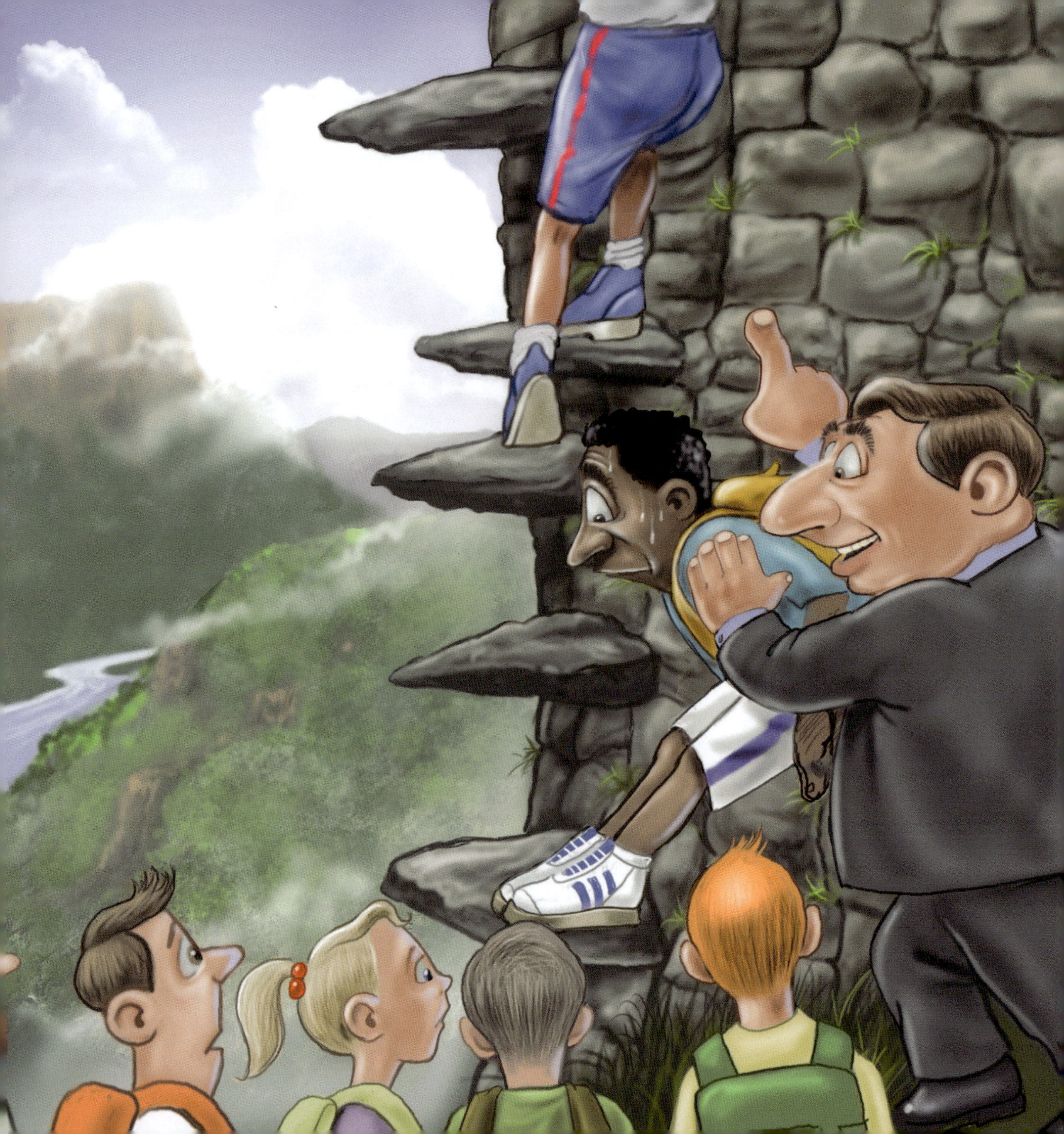

Buzzwords & BS | Stephen Kirlew

"STRATEGIC STAIRCASE"

The Origin

Although the origin is unknown, the 'strategic staircase' framework of bridging the gap between strategy and action is a popular business process. Given the choice, I always opt for the elevator.

The Meaning

Quite simply, a 'strategic staircase' is a business plan of action that presents a step by step pathway to success for a company to follow.

Bob Sheldon says...

"And that concludes our walkthrough of the strategic staircase. Does that count as my cardio for the day?"

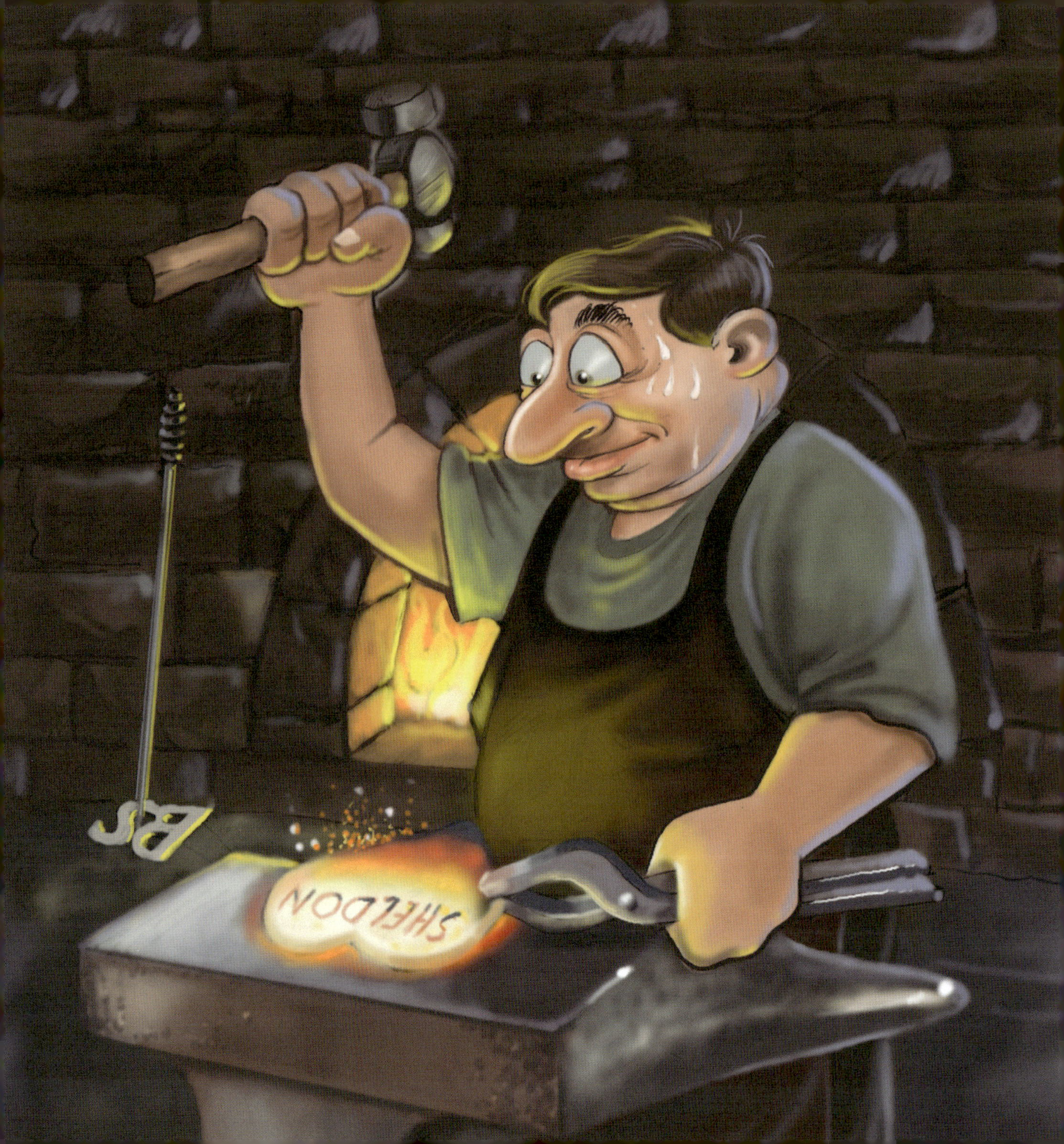
BS
SHELDON

Buzzwords & BS | Stephen Kirlew

"STRIKE WHILE THE IRON IS HOT"

The Origin

This phrase harks back to an age of blacksmiths who would heat iron, then strike it with a hammer to change the shape. If they hit too soon or too late the iron would be the wrong temperature and the chance to shape it would be lost.

The Meaning

To 'strike while the iron is hot' in a business setting is to take immediate action to seize an opportunity before it's too late.

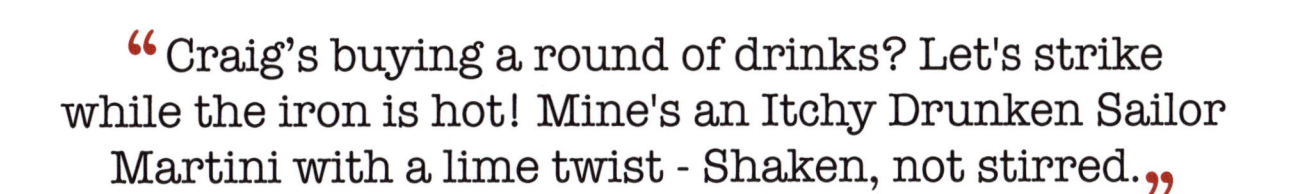

Bob Sheldon says…

"Craig's buying a round of drinks? Let's strike while the iron is hot! Mine's an Itchy Drunken Sailor Martini with a lime twist - Shaken, not stirred."

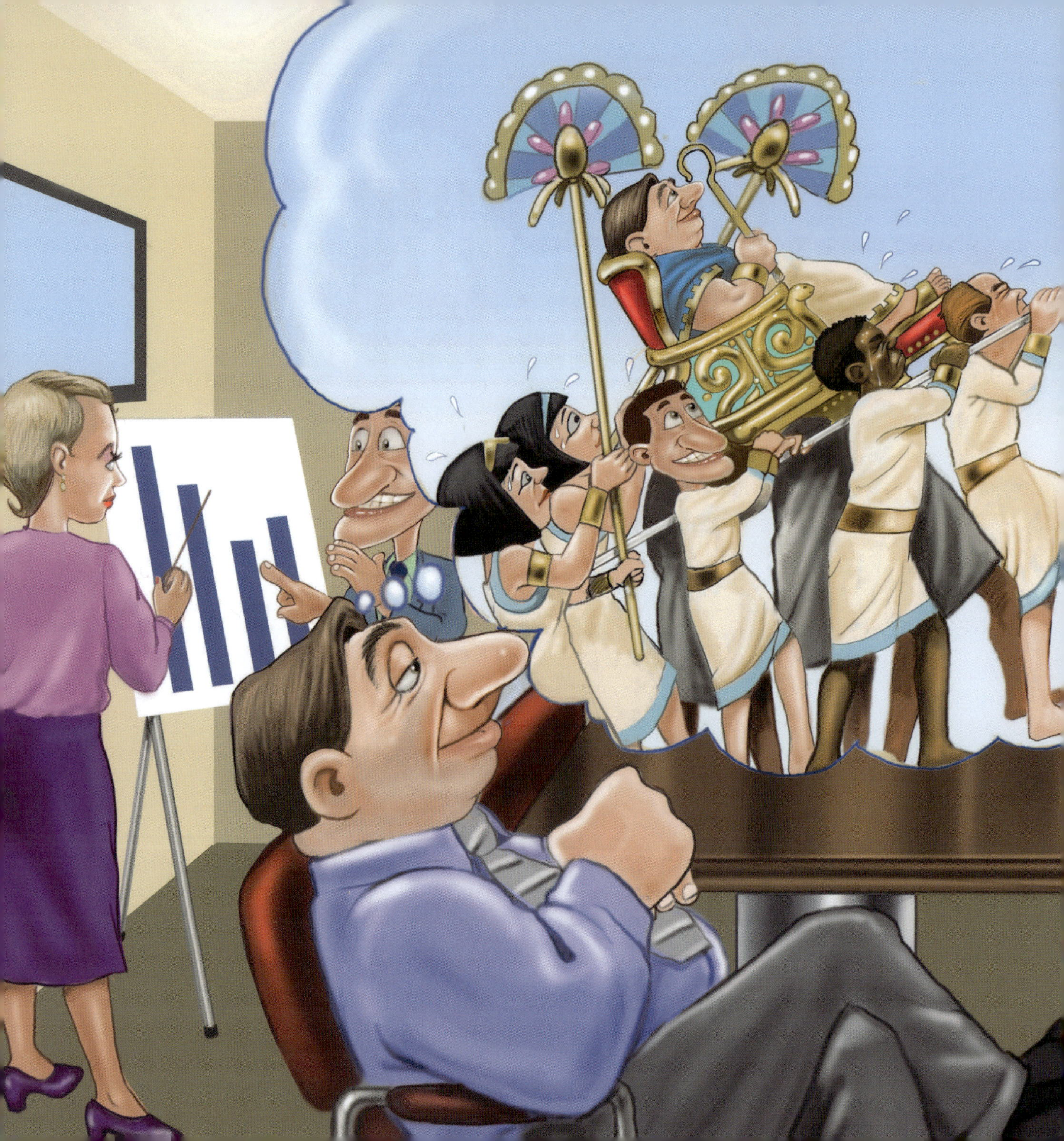

Buzzwords & BS | Stephen Kirlew

"SWEAT EQUITY"

The Origin
This phrase was originally used in the 1930s to refer to unpaid labor in the construction industry contributing to an increase in house prices.

The Meaning
In modern times, 'sweat equity' refers to the unpaid or additional time and effort put into a project or start-up, often in exchange for an equity stake in lieu of salary.

Bob Sheldon says...

> "I've built up so much sweat equity over the years, today I'm a millionaire. And I did it without even breaking a sweat."

0101

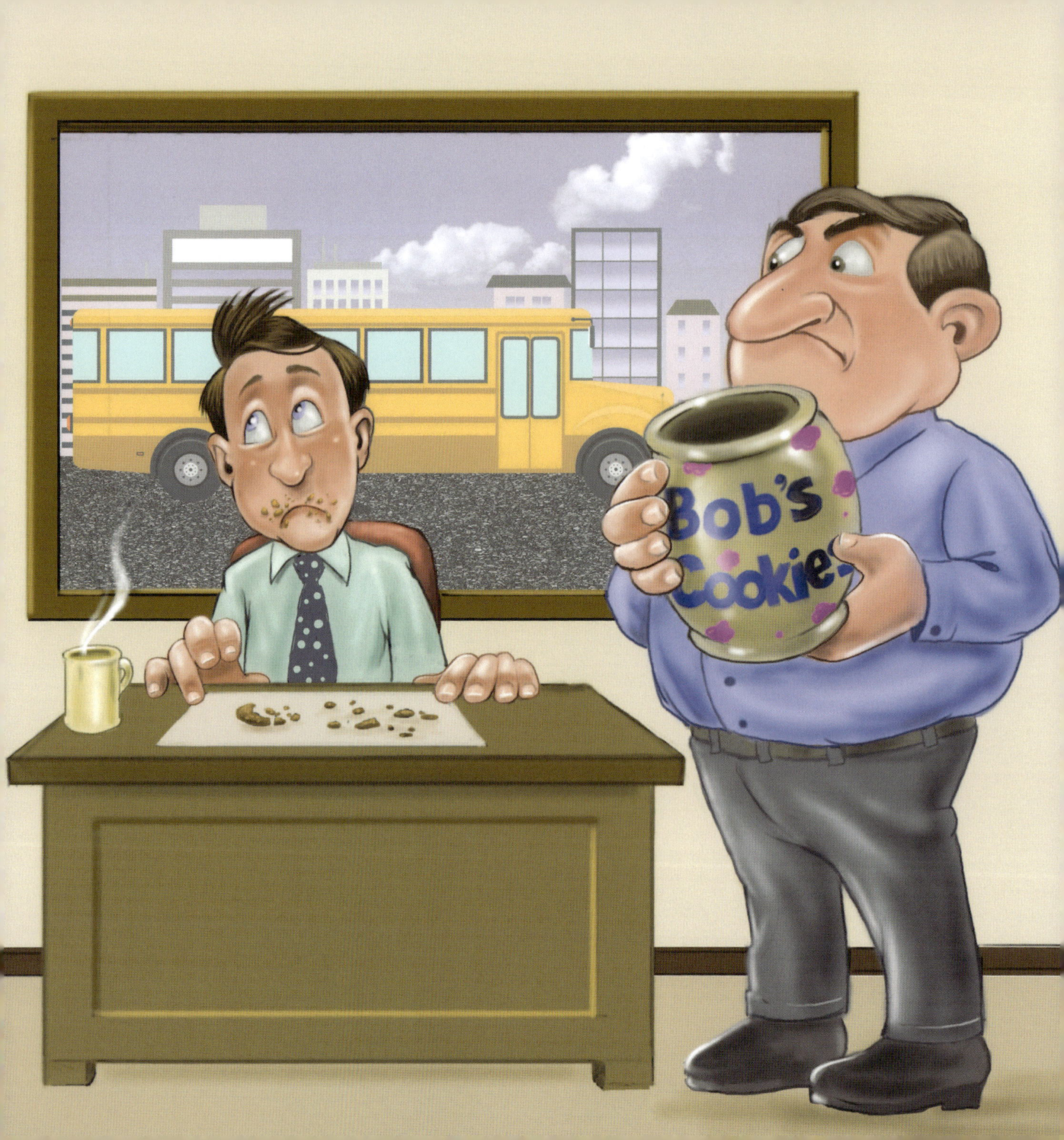
Bob's Cookies

Buzzwords & BS | Stephen Kirlew

"THROW UNDER THE BUS"

The Origin

This rather unpleasant phrase derives from British politics where it describes an ill-timed act of misfortune.

As Churchill said, the difference between politics and war is you can be killed many times in politics.

The Meaning

You're in for a bumpy ride if this phrase is used in a business setting as it means to betray or sacrifice someone to advance your career or best interests.

Bob Sheldon says...

" You weren't thrown under the bus for the poor sales figures, Junior; you've been identified as the office cookie thief. "

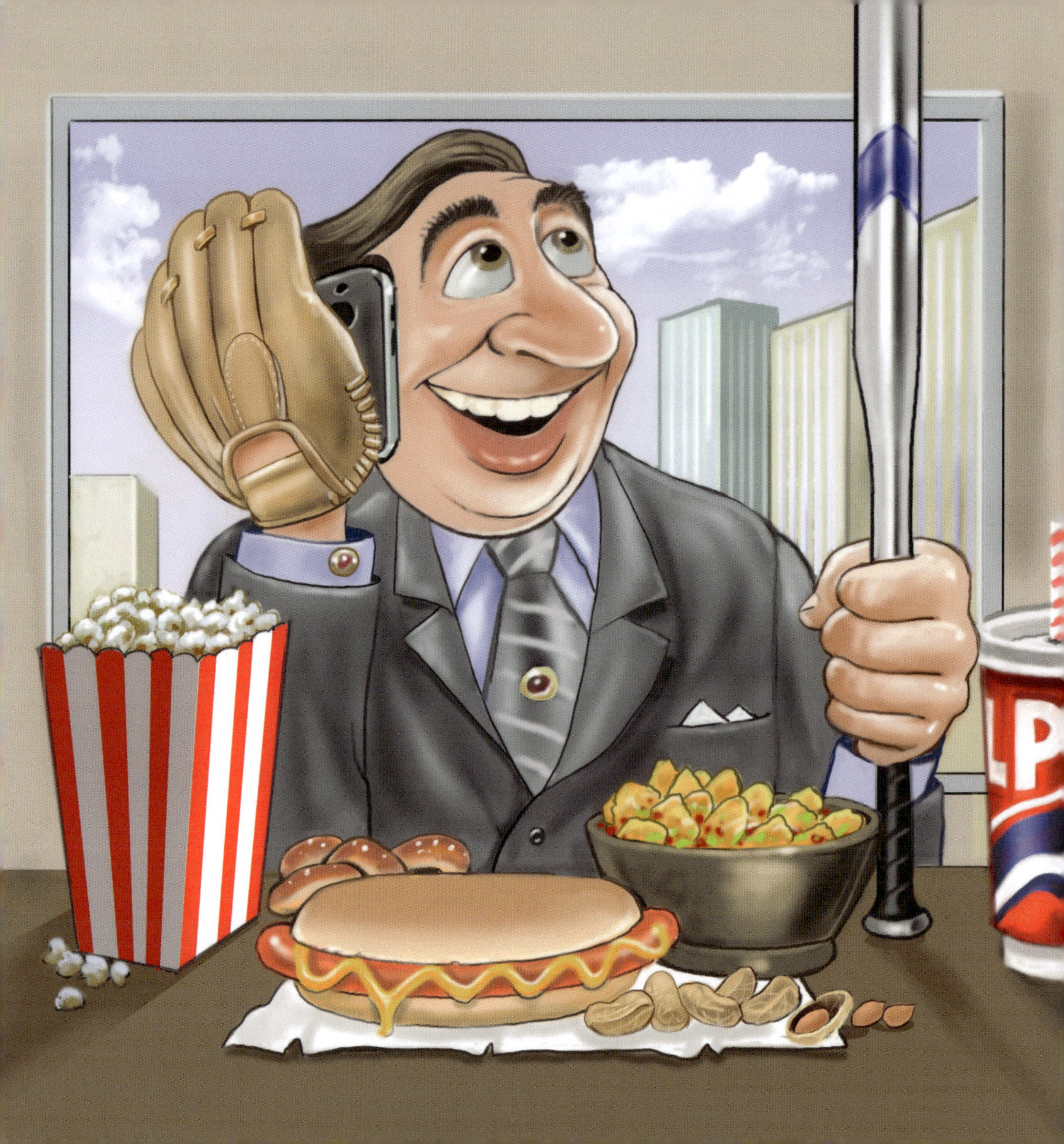

Buzzwords & BS | Stephen Kirlew

"TOUCH BASE"

The Origin
Described by philosopher Morris Raphael Cohen as America's national religion, baseball is the source of this buzzword as both runners and fielders have to physically touch the base to be safe or record an out.

The Meaning
Heard in offices worldwide on an almost daily basis, this overused buzzword means to make contact, reconnect, or communicate with someone.

Bob Sheldon says...

" I'm just calling to touch base. Yeah, I know you're sitting outside my office, Sheree. Can I have a cup of coffee please? "

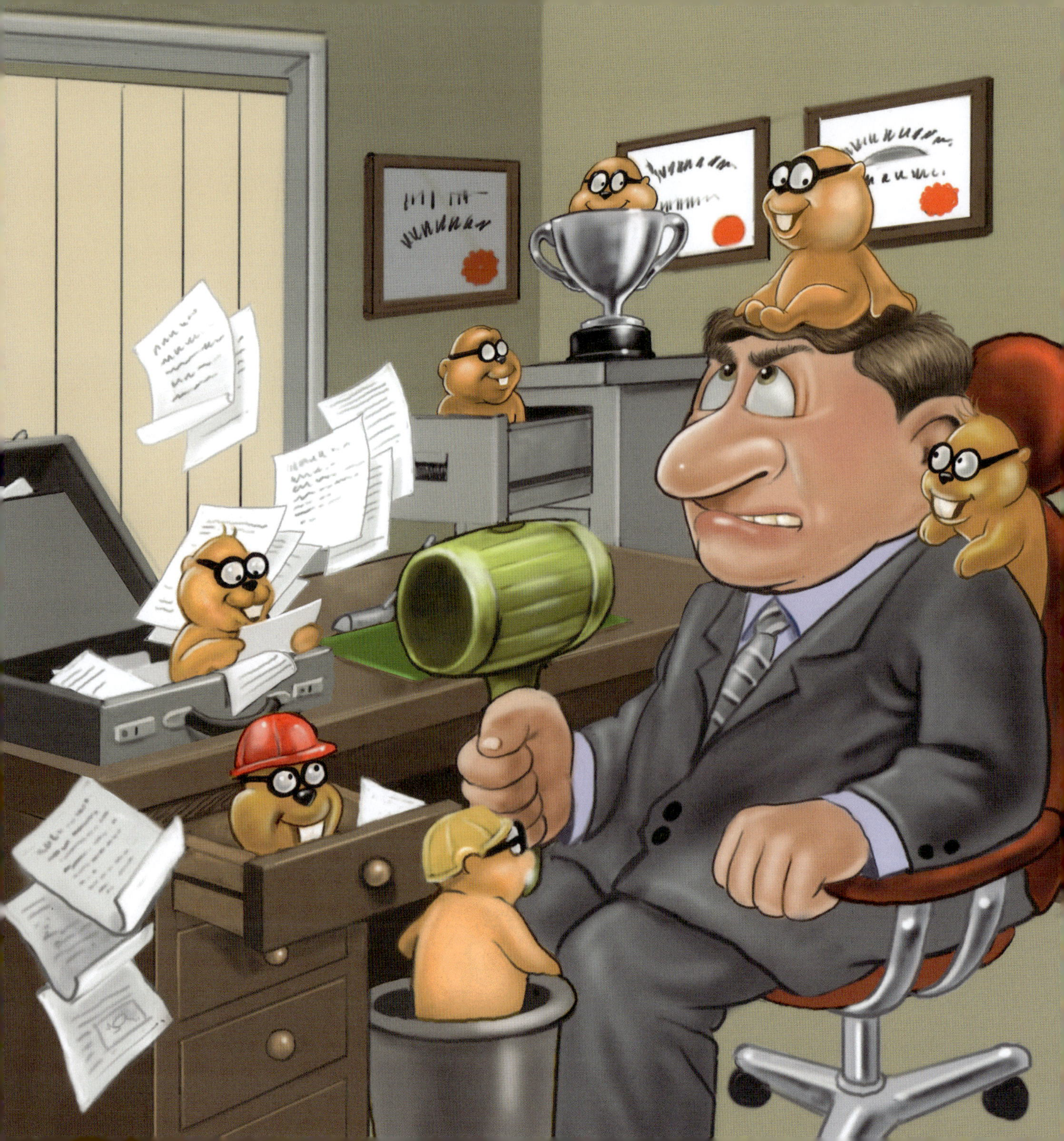

"WHAC-A-MOLE"

The Origin

This buzzword relates to the popular 70s arcade game 'Whac-A-Mole' which involved repeatedly hitting mechanical moles as they popped up from holes. It's not related to The Southlander's '50s hit "I Am A Mole And I Live In a Hole". You'll have that song in your head all day now.

The Meaning

This jargon means you're repeatedly dealing with one issue after the next. Once you solve one problem, another suddenly appears. A good--albeit annoying--example is closing pop-up windows that keep appearing when browsing the web.

Bob Sheldon says...

"Managing Jason is like whac-a-mole. As soon as you fix one problem, another appears. And he's very hairy... like a mole."

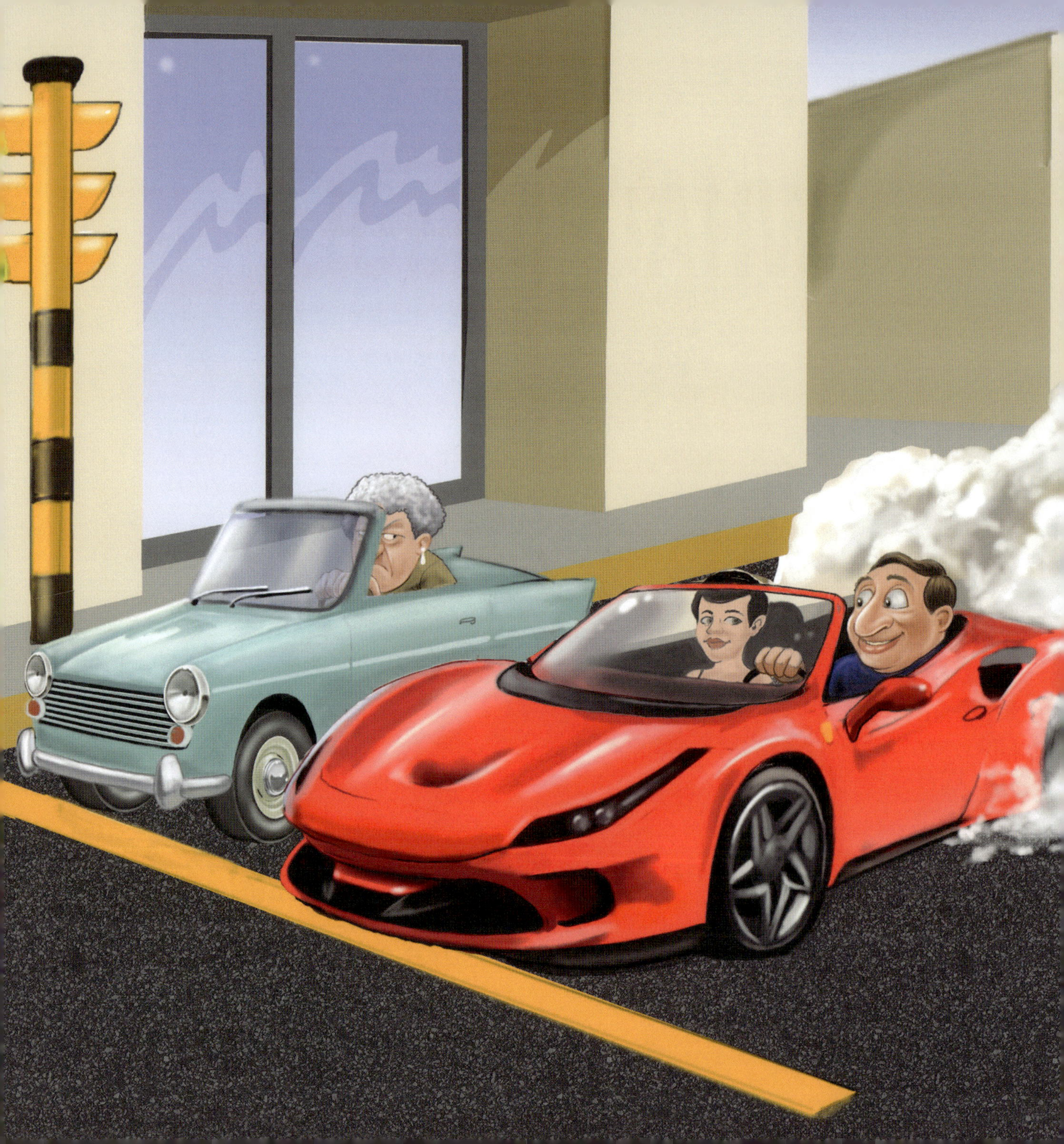

Buzzwords & BS | Stephen Kirlew

"WHERE THE RUBBER MEETS THE ROAD"

The Origin

This expression refers to the point at which a rubber tire connects with the road. Why did I resign from my job in a car shop repairing punctures? I was 'tired'. Get it?!

The Meaning

In a business setting, this is the crucial moment at which an idea, product or theory is put to the test to see if it works.

Bob Sheldon says...

"We deploy tomorrow, team, so that's when the rubber meets the road. Which reminds me. I'll be in late tomorrow. I'm test driving a Lamborghini Urus."

PLAY BOB'S BUZZWORD BINGO!

Ease the buzzword boredom with Bob's Buzzword Bingo! See if you can complete a full line (horizontal or vertical)!

Buzzwords & BS | Stephen Kirlew

BINGO!

30,000 FOOT VIEW	CHANGE AGENT	FLAVOR OF THE MONTH	OPEN THE KIMONO	SILVER BULLET
BANDWIDTH	DEEP DIVE	HERDING CATS	PIGGYBACK	SHOW PONY
BITE THE BULLET	DRINKING THE KOOL-AID	IN THE WEEDS	PUSHING ROPE	STATISTICAL MASSAGE
BOIL THE OCEAN	DRINKING FROM THE FIREHOSE	LOW HANGING FRUIT	PUT TO BED	STRIKE WHILE THE IRON IS HOT
CIRCLE BACK	DUCKS IN A ROW	MOVE THE NEEDLE	ROADMAP	TOUCH BASE

CONGRATULATIONS

Your Bob Sheldon education is now complete.

Now hit those boardrooms and spread the word — the Buzzword!

...But maybe lay off the BS?

Printed in Great Britain
by Amazon

ALABASTER

⚱ ALABASTER

© 2016 Alabaster Co.

All rights reserved.
No part of this publication may be reproduced, distributed or transmitted in any form or by any means, including photocopying or other electronic or mechanical method, without prior written permission of the editor, except in the case of brief quotations embodied in critical reviews and certain other noncommercial uses permitted by copyright law. For permission requests, please write to us.

Holy Bible, New Living Translation, copyright © 1996, 2004, 2015 by Tyndale House Foundation. Used by permission of Tyndale House Publishers, Inc. All rights reserved.

Printed in Canada

Contact
hello@alabasterco.com
www.alabasterco.com

Alabaster Co. The Bible Beautiful.
Visual imagery & thoughtful design integrated within the four Gospels.
Cultivating conversation between art, beauty, & faith.

Founded in 2016.

NLT

ARTIST INTRODUCTION

At its core, the Gospel of Mark is the story of Jesus as the suffering-servant. In a pivotal moment during his ministry, Jesus tells Peter and the crowd that the "Son of Man must suffer many terrible things" and eventually be killed, an idea radically different from whom people thought the "victorious" Messiah was foretold to be. Jesus declares those who try to save their life will lose it, and those who lose their life for His sake will save it.

We were immediately struck by the strength and directness of Jesus' tone. Yet hidden within his words, we found a fragment of his love. Jesus does not appear as a conqueror with the purpose of establishing an empire, but as a suffering servant willing to do anything for the sake of loving the other, even if it means death.

In a culture dominated by a desire to climb to the top and profit no matter the cost, Jesus offers an alternative narrative, one where a life is not measured by what one accomplishes, but how one chooses to love through suffering.

This suffering-love anchors our creative foundation for Mark. We thread Mark with hints of red, a color that dominates our culture's visual language of love. Our images - more than in any other gospel - are not tied to one another but instead stand on their own. This is for two reasons. First, we honor the fact that this is not only the shortest Gospel, but perhaps also the most punctual.

And second, we acknowledge - especially in our personal experience - that to walk in the suffering-love of God is never neatly laid out. There are breaks, and confusions, and ups and downs. It takes a lifetime of honesty to somehow piece it all together. Here is The Gospel of Mark.

Bryan Chung and Brian Chung

GOSPEL OF MARK

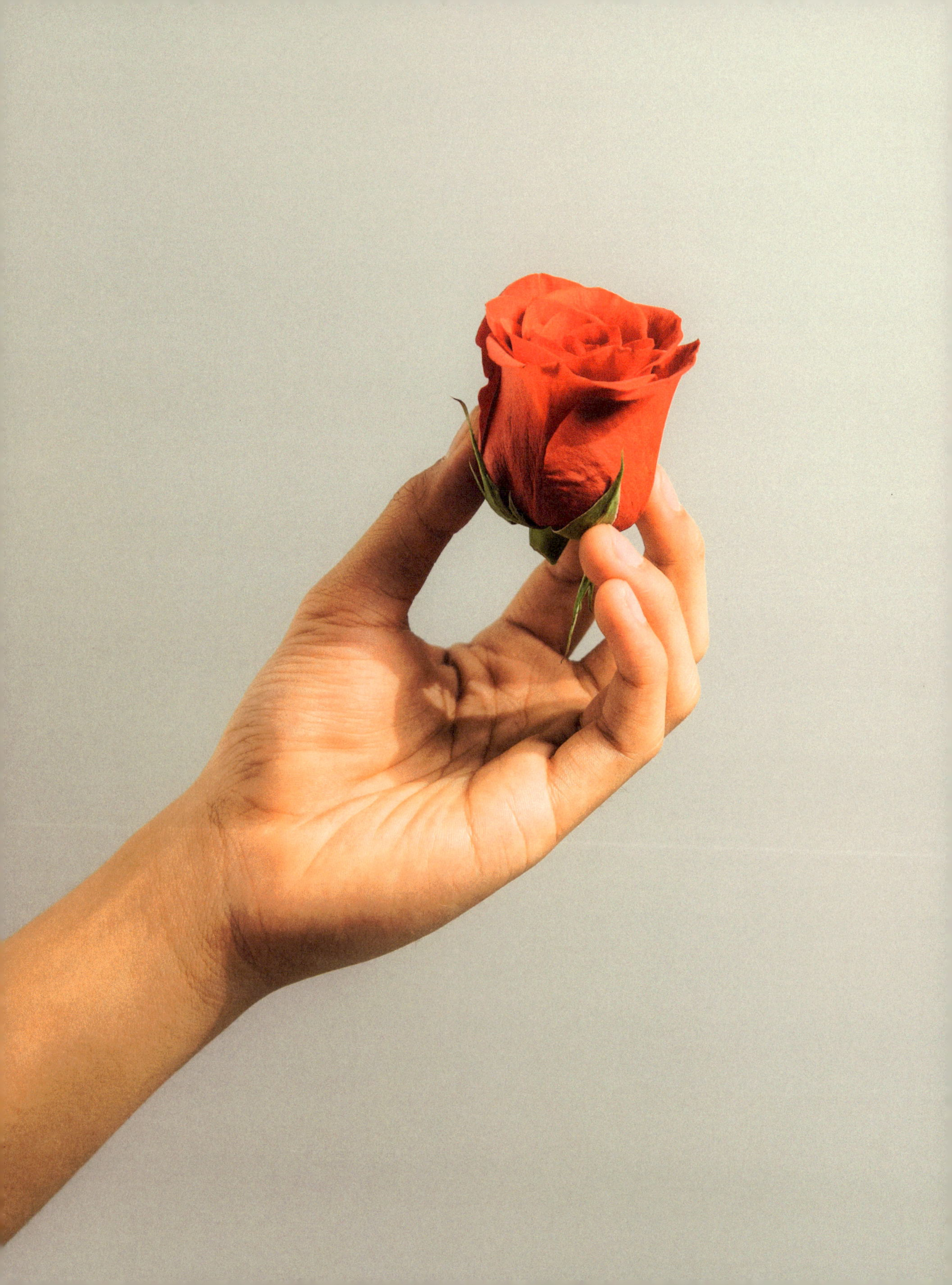

1

JOHN THE BAPTIST PREPARES THE WAY

This is the Good News about Jesus the Messiah, the Son of God. It began ² just as the prophet Isaiah had written: "Look, I am sending my messenger ahead of you, and he will prepare your way. ³ He is a voice shouting in the wilderness, 'Prepare the way for the Lord's coming! Clear the road for him!'" ⁴ This messenger was John the Baptist. He was in the wilderness and preached that people should be baptized to show that they had repented of their sins and turned to God to be forgiven. ⁵ All of Judea, including all the people of Jerusalem, went out to see and hear John. And when they confessed their sins, he baptized them in the Jordan River. ⁶ His clothes were woven from coarse camel hair, and he wore a leather belt around his waist. For food he ate locusts and wild honey. ⁷ John announced: "Someone is coming soon who is greater than I am—so much greater that I'm not even worthy to stoop down like a slave and untie the straps of his sandals. ⁸ I baptize you with water, but he will baptize you with the Holy Spirit!"

THE BAPTISM AND TEMPTATION OF JESUS

⁹ One day Jesus came from Nazareth in Galilee, and John baptized him in the Jordan River. ¹⁰ As Jesus came up out of the water, he saw the heavens splitting apart and the Holy Spirit descending on him like a dove. ¹¹ And a voice from heaven said, "You are my dearly loved Son, and you bring me great joy." ¹² The Spirit then compelled Jesus to go into the wilderness, ¹³ where he was tempted by Satan for forty days. He was out among the wild animals, and angels took care of him. ¹⁴ Later on, after John was arrested, Jesus went into Galilee, where he preached God's Good News. ¹⁵ "The time promised by God has come at last!" he announced. "The Kingdom of God is near! Repent of your sins and believe the Good News!"

THE FIRST DISCIPLES

[16] One day as Jesus was walking along the shore of the Sea of Galilee, he saw Simon and his brother Andrew throwing a net into the water, for they fished for a living. [17] Jesus called out to them, "Come, follow me, and I will show you how to fish for people!" [18] And they left their nets at once and followed him. [19] A little farther up the shore Jesus saw Zebedee's sons, James and John, in a boat repairing their nets. [20] He called them at once, and they also followed him, leaving their father, Zebedee, in the boat with the hired men.

JESUS CASTS OUT AN EVIL SPIRIT

[21] Jesus and his companions went to the town of Capernaum. When the Sabbath day came, he went into the synagogue and began to teach. [22] The people were amazed at his teaching, for he taught with real authority—quite unlike the teachers of religious law. [23] Suddenly, a man in the synagogue who was possessed by an evil spirit cried out, [24] "Why are you interfering with us, Jesus of Nazareth? Have you come to destroy us? I know who you are—the Holy One of God!" [25] But Jesus reprimanded him. "Be quiet! Come out of the man," he ordered. [26] At that, the evil spirit screamed, threw the man into a convulsion, and then came out of him. [27] Amazement gripped the audience, and they began to discuss what had happened. "What sort of new teaching is this?" they asked excitedly. "It has such authority! Even evil spirits obey his orders!" [28] The news about Jesus spread quickly throughout the entire region of Galilee.

JESUS HEALS MANY PEOPLE

[29] After Jesus left the synagogue with James and John, they went to Simon and Andrew's home. [30] Now Simon's mother-in-law was sick in bed with a high fever. They told Jesus about her right away. [31] So he went to her bedside, took her by the hand, and helped her sit up. Then the fever left her, and she prepared a meal for them. [32] That evening after sunset, many sick and demon-possessed people were brought to Jesus. [33] The whole town gathered at the door to watch. [34] So Jesus healed many people who were sick with various diseases, and he cast out many demons. But because the demons knew who he was, he did not allow them to speak.

JESUS PREACHES IN GALILEE

[35] Before daybreak the next morning, Jesus got up and went out to an isolated place to pray. [36] Later Simon and the others went out to find him. [37] When they found him, they said, "Everyone is looking for you." [38] But Jesus replied, "We must go on to other towns as well, and I will preach to them, too. That is why I came." [39] So he traveled throughout the region of Galilee, preaching in the synagogues and casting out demons.

JESUS HEALS A MAN WITH LEPROSY

[40] A man with leprosy came and knelt in front of Jesus, begging to be healed. "If you are willing, you can heal me and make me clean," he said. [41] Moved with compassion, Jesus reached out and touched him. "I am willing," he said. "Be healed!" [42] Instantly the leprosy disappeared, and the man was healed. [43] Then Jesus sent him on his way with a stern warning: [44] "Don't tell anyone about this. Instead, go to the priest and let him examine you. Take along the offering required in the law of Moses for those who have been healed of leprosy. This will be a public testimony that you have been cleansed." [45] But the man went and spread the word, proclaiming to everyone what had happened. As a result, large crowds soon surrounded Jesus, and he couldn't publicly enter a town anywhere. He had to stay out in the secluded places, but people from everywhere kept coming to him.

CHAPTER 1

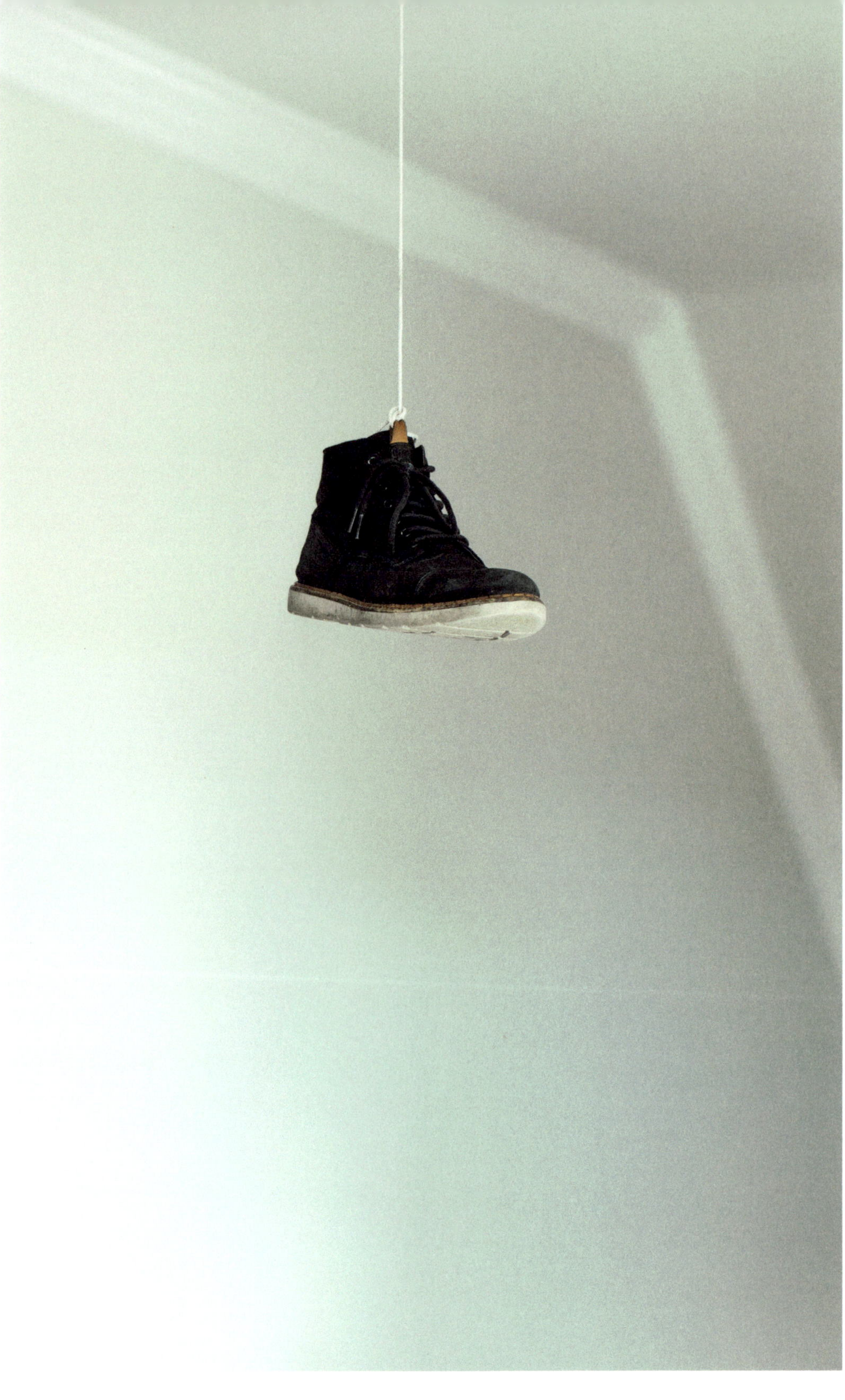

2

JESUS HEALS A PARALYZED MAN

When Jesus returned to Capernaum several days later, the news spread quickly that he was back home. [2] Soon the house where he was staying was so packed with visitors that there was no more room, even outside the door. While he was preaching God's word to them, [3] four men arrived carrying a paralyzed man on a mat. [4] They couldn't bring him to Jesus because of the crowd, so they dug a hole through the roof above his head. Then they lowered the man on his mat, right down in front of Jesus. [5] Seeing their faith, Jesus said to the paralyzed man, "My child, your sins are forgiven." [6] But some of the teachers of religious law who were sitting there thought to themselves, [7] "What is he saying? This is blasphemy! Only God can forgive sins!" [8] Jesus knew immediately what they were thinking, so he asked them, "Why do you question this in your hearts? [9] Is it easier to say to the paralyzed man 'Your sins are forgiven,' or 'Stand up, pick up your mat, and walk'? [10] So I will prove to you that the Son of Man has the authority on earth to forgive sins." Then Jesus turned to the paralyzed man and said, [11] "Stand up, pick up your mat, and go home!" [12] And the man jumped up, grabbed his mat, and walked out through the stunned onlookers. They were all amazed and praised God, exclaiming, "We've never seen anything like this before!"

JESUS CALLS LEVI

[13] Then Jesus went out to the lakeshore again and taught the crowds that were coming to him. [14] As he walked along, he saw Levi son of Alphaeus sitting at his tax collector's booth. "Follow me and be my disciple," Jesus said to him. So Levi got up and followed him. [15] Later, Levi invited Jesus and his disciples to his home as dinner guests, along with many tax collectors and other disreputable sinners. (There were many people of this kind among Jesus' followers.) [16] But when the teachers of religious law who were Pharisees saw him eating with tax collectors and other sinners, they asked his disciples, "Why does he eat with such scum?" [17] When Jesus heard this, he told them, "Healthy people don't need a doctor—sick people do. I have come to call not those who think they are righteous, but those who know they are sinners."

A DISCUSSION ABOUT FASTING

[18] Once when John's disciples and the Pharisees were fasting, some people came to Jesus and asked, "Why don't your disciples fast like John's disciples and the Pharisees do?" [19] Jesus replied, "Do wedding guests fast while celebrating with the groom? Of course not. They can't fast while the groom is with them. [20] But someday the groom will be taken away from them, and then they will fast. [21] "Besides, who would patch old clothing with new cloth? For the new patch would shrink and rip away from the old cloth, leaving an even bigger tear than before. [22] "And no one puts new wine into old wineskins. For the wine would burst the wineskins, and the wine and the skins would both be lost. New wine calls for new wineskins."

A DISCUSSION ABOUT THE SABBATH

[23] One Sabbath day as Jesus was walking through some grainfields, his disciples began breaking off heads of grain to eat. [24] But the Pharisees said to Jesus, "Look, why are they breaking the law by harvesting grain on the Sabbath?" [25] Jesus said to them, "Haven't you ever read in the Scriptures what David did when he and his companions were hungry? [26] He went into the house of God (during the days when Abiathar was high priest) and broke the law by eating the sacred loaves of bread that only the priests are allowed to eat. He also gave some to his companions." [27] Then Jesus said to them, "The Sabbath was made to meet the needs of people, and not people to meet the requirements of the Sabbath. [28] So the Son of Man is Lord, even over the Sabbath!

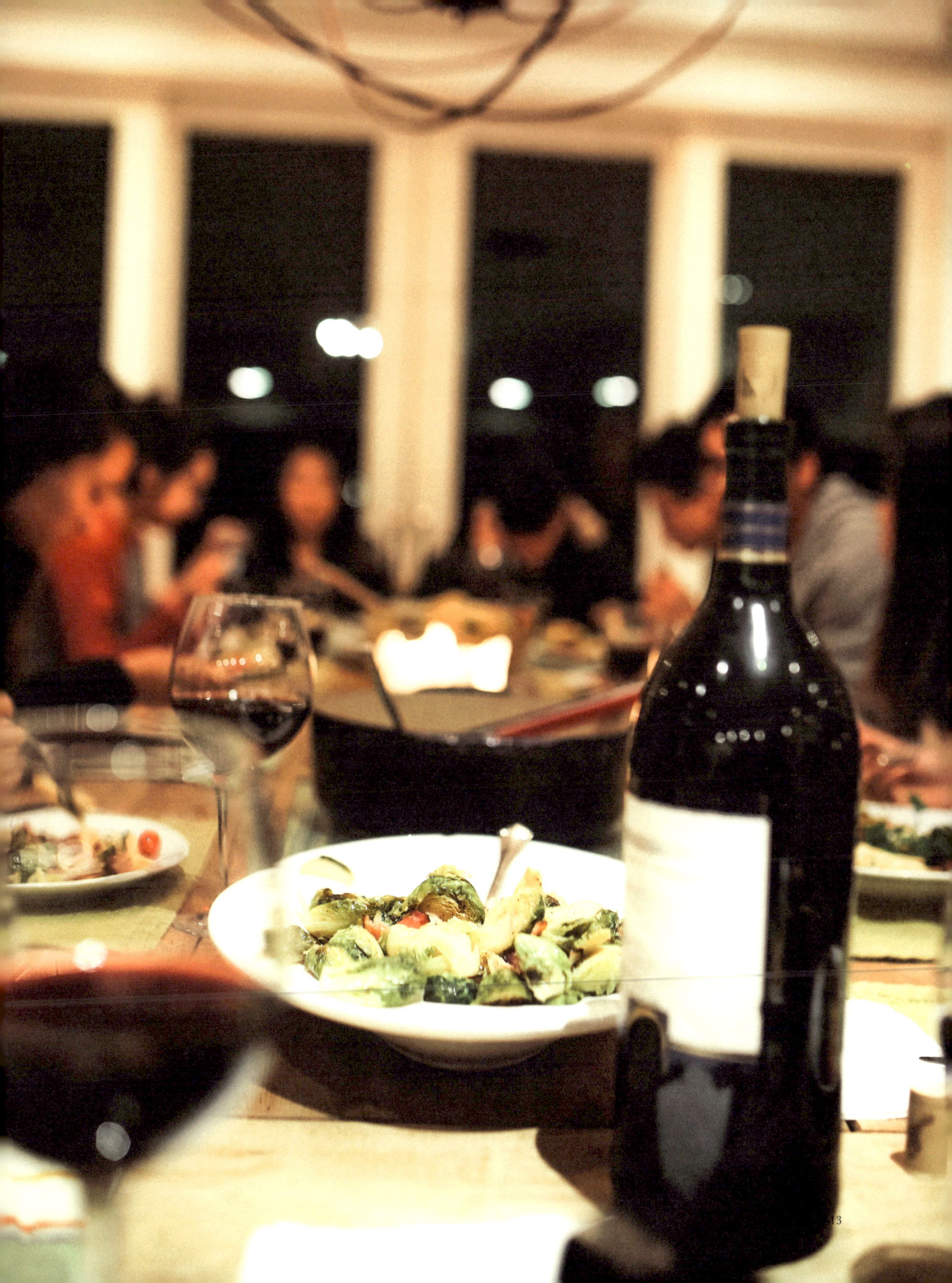

3

JESUS HEALS ON THE SABBATH

[1] Jesus went into the synagogue again and noticed a man with a deformed hand. [2] Since it was the Sabbath, Jesus' enemies watched him closely. If he healed the man's hand, they planned to accuse him of working on the Sabbath. [3] Jesus said to the man with the deformed hand, "Come and stand in front of everyone." [4] Then he turned to his critics and asked, "Does the law permit good deeds on the Sabbath, or is it a day for doing evil? Is this a day to save life or to destroy it?" But they wouldn't answer him. [5] He looked around at them angrily and was deeply saddened by their hard hearts. Then he said to the man, "Hold out your hand." So the man held out his hand, and it was restored! [6] At once the Pharisees went away and met with the supporters of Herod to plot how to kill Jesus.

CROWDS FOLLOW JESUS

[7] Jesus went out to the lake with his disciples, and a large crowd followed him. They came from all over Galilee, Judea, [8] Jerusalem, Idumea, from east of the Jordan River, and even from as far north as Tyre and Sidon. The news about his miracles had spread far and wide, and vast numbers of people came to see him. [9] Jesus instructed his disciples to have a boat ready so the crowd would not crush him. [10] He had healed many people that day, so all the sick people eagerly pushed forward to touch him. [11] And whenever those possessed by evil spirits caught sight of him, the spirits would throw them to the ground in front of him shrieking, "You are the Son of God!" [12] But Jesus sternly commanded the spirits not to reveal who he was.

JESUS CHOOSES THE TWELVE DISCIPLES

[13] Afterward Jesus went up on a mountain and called out the ones he wanted to go with him. And they came to him. [14] Then he appointed twelve of them and called them his apostles. They were to accompany him, and he would send them out to preach, [15] giving them authority to cast out demons. [16] These are the twelve he chose: Simon (whom he named Peter), [17] James and John (the sons of Zebedee, but Jesus nicknamed them "Sons of Thunder"), [18] Andrew, Philip, Bartholomew, Matthew, Thomas, James (son of Alphaeus), Thaddaeus, Simon (the zealot), [19] Judas Iscariot (who later betrayed him).

JESUS AND THE PRINCE OF DEMONS

[20] One time Jesus entered a house, and the crowds began to gather again. Soon he and his disciples couldn't even find time to eat. [21] When his family heard what was happening, they tried to take him away. "He's out of his mind," they said. [22] But the teachers of religious law who had arrived from Jerusalem said, "He's possessed by Satan, the prince of demons. That's where he gets the power to cast out demons." [23] Jesus called them over and responded with an illustration. "How can Satan cast out Satan?" he asked. [24] "A kingdom divided by civil war will collapse. [25] Similarly, a family splintered by feuding will fall apart. [26] And if Satan is divided and fights against himself, how can he stand? He would never survive. [27] Let me illustrate this further. Who is powerful enough to enter the house of a strong man and plunder his goods? Only someone even stronger—someone who could tie him up and then plunder his house. [28] "I tell you the truth, all sin and blasphemy can be forgiven, [29] but anyone who blasphemes the Holy Spirit will never be forgiven. This is a sin with eternal consequences." [30] He told them this because they were saying, "He's possessed by an evil spirit."

THE TRUE FAMILY OF JESUS

[31] Then Jesus' mother and brothers came to see him. They stood outside and sent word for him to come out and talk with them. [32] There was a crowd sitting around Jesus, and someone said, "Your mother and your brothers are outside asking for you." [33] Jesus replied, "Who is my mother? Who are my brothers?" [34] Then he looked at those around him and said, "Look, these are my mother and brothers. [35] Anyone who does God's will is my brother and sister and mother."

CHAPTER 3

4

PARABLE OF THE FARMER SCATTERING SEEDS

Once again Jesus began teaching by the lakeshore. A very large crowd soon gathered around him, so he got into a boat. Then he sat in the boat while all the people remained on the shore. [2] He taught them by telling many stories in the form of parables, such as this one: [3] "Listen! A farmer went out to plant some seed. [4] As he scattered it across his field, some of the seed fell on a footpath, and the birds came and ate it. [5] Other seed fell on shallow soil with underlying rock. [6] But the plant soon wilted under the hot sun, and since it didn't have deep roots, it died. [7] Other seed fell among thorns that grew up and choked out the tender plants so they produced no grain. [8] Still other seeds fell on fertile soil, and they sprouted, grew, and produced a crop that was thirty, sixty, and even a hundred times as much as had been planted!" [9] Then he said, "Anyone with ears to hear should listen and understand." [10] Later, when Jesus was alone with the twelve disciples and with the others who were gathered around, they asked him what the parables meant. [11] He replied, "You are permitted to understand the secret of the Kingdom of God. But I use parables for everything I say to outsiders, [12] so that the Scriptures might be fulfilled: 'When they see what I do, they will learn nothing. When they hear what I say, they will not understand. Otherwise, they will turn to me and be forgiven.'" [13] Then Jesus said to them, "If you can't understand the meaning of this parable, how will you understand all the other parables? [14] The farmer plants seed by taking God's word to others. [15] The seed that fell on the footpath represents those who hear the message, only to have Satan come at once and take it away. [16] The seed on the rocky soil represents those who hear the message and immediately receive it with joy. [17] But since they don't have deep roots, they don't last long. They fall away as soon as they have problems or are persecuted for believing God's word. [18] The seed that fell among the thorns represents others who hear God's word, [19] but all too quickly the message is crowded out by the worries of this life, the lure of wealth, and the desire for other things, so no fruit is produced. [20] And the seed that fell on good soil represents those who hear and accept God's word and produce a harvest of thirty, sixty, or even a hundred times as much as had been planted!"

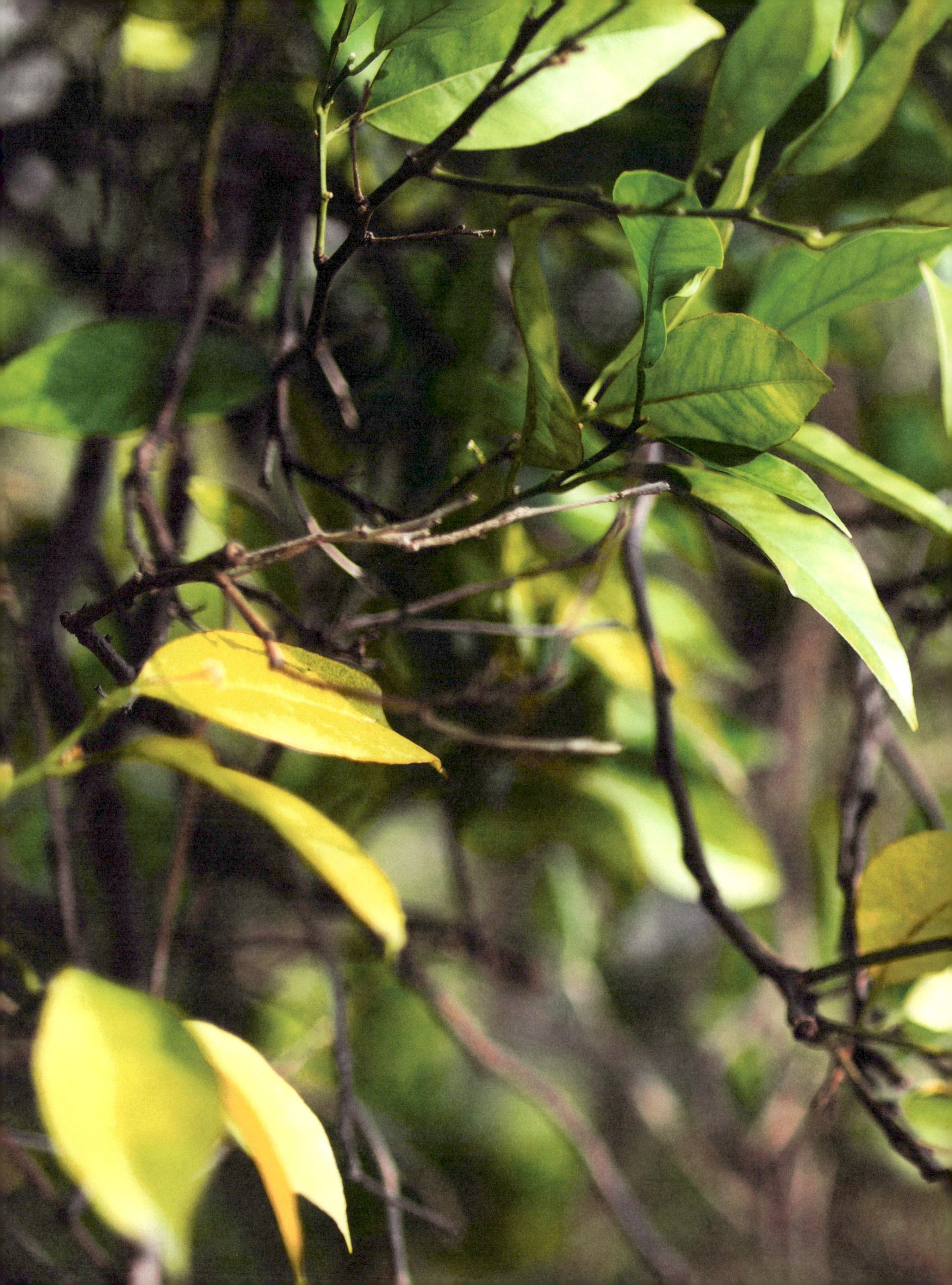

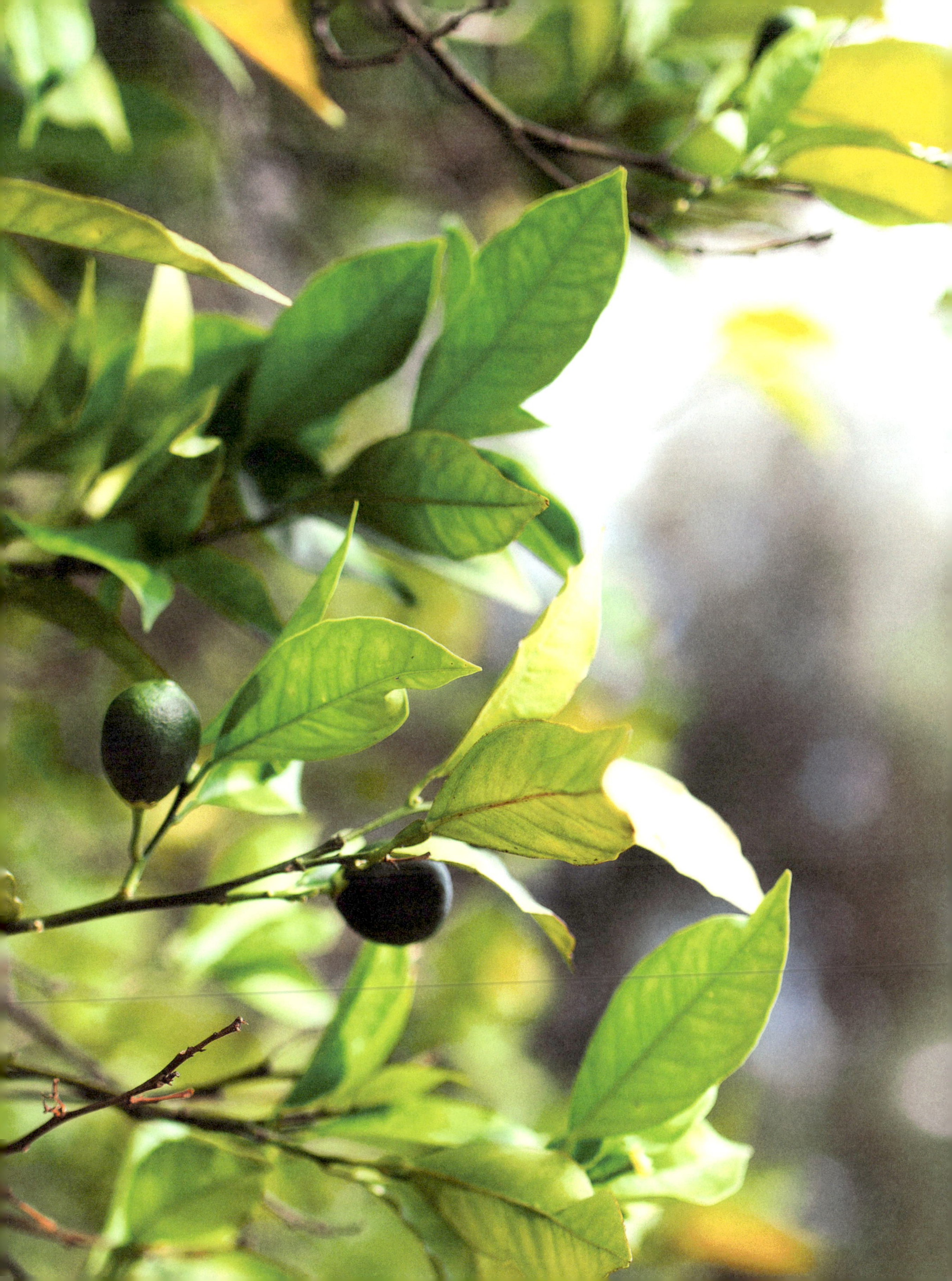

ALABASTER | GOSPEL OF MARK

PARABLE OF THE LAMP

²¹ Then Jesus asked them, "Would anyone light a lamp and then put it under a basket or under a bed? Of course not! A lamp is placed on a stand, where its light will shine. ²² For everything that is hidden will eventually be brought into the open, and every secret will be brought to light. ²³ Anyone with ears to hear should listen and understand." ²⁴ Then he added, "Pay close attention to what you hear. The closer you listen, the more understanding you will be given—and you will receive even more. ²⁵ To those who listen to my teaching, more understanding will be given. But for those who are not listening, even what little understanding they have will be taken away from them."

PARABLE OF THE GROWING SEED

²⁶ Jesus also said, "The Kingdom of God is like a farmer who scatters seed on the ground. ²⁷ Night and day, while he's asleep or awake, the seed sprouts and grows, but he does not understand how it happens. ²⁸ The earth produces the crops on its own. First a leaf blade pushes through, then the heads of wheat are formed, and finally the grain ripens. ²⁹ And as soon as the grain is ready, the farmer comes and harvests it with a sickle, for the harvest time has come.

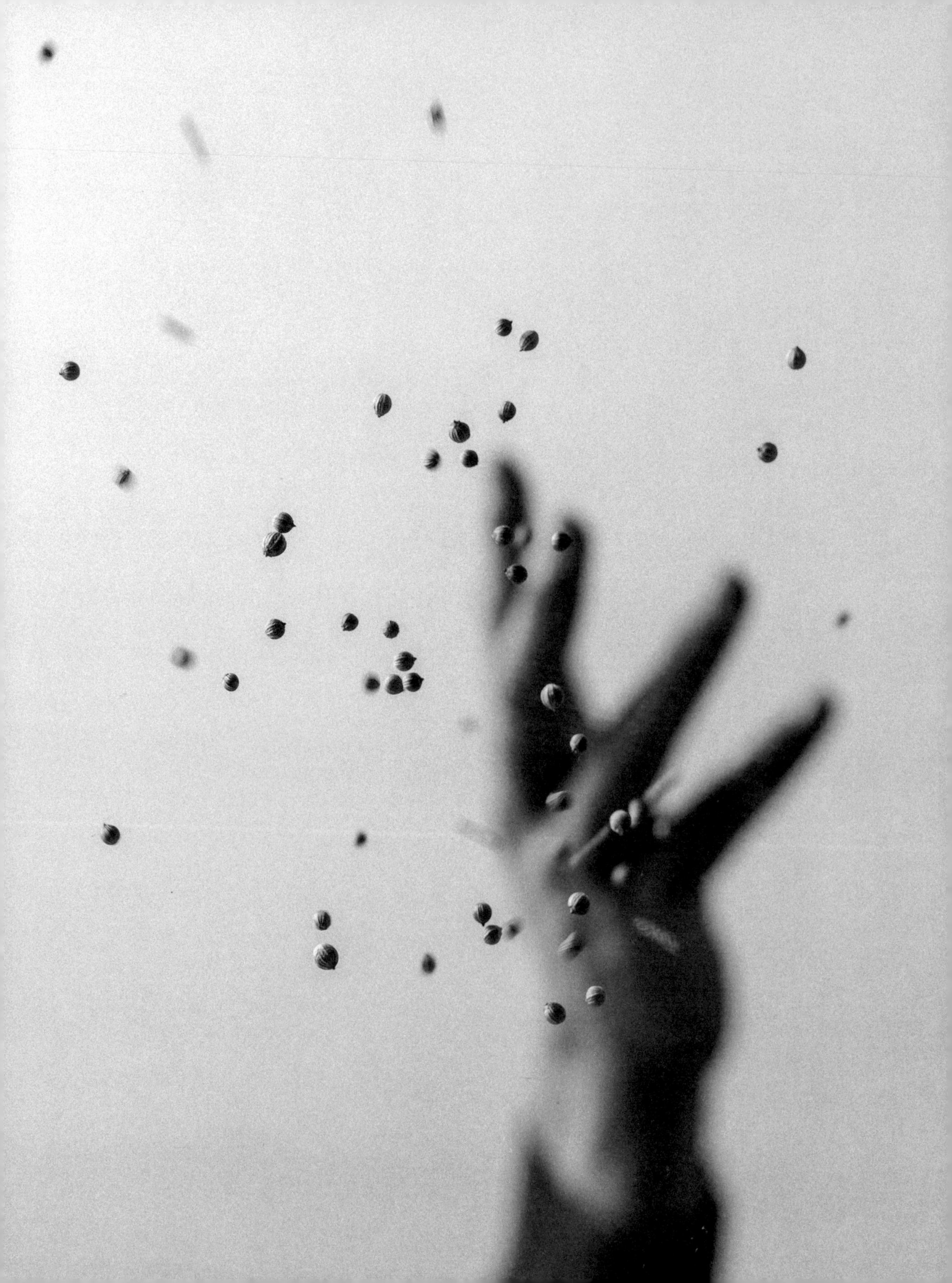

PARABLE OF THE MUSTARD SEED

[30] Jesus said, "How can I describe the Kingdom of God? What story should I use to illustrate it? [31] It is like a mustard seed planted in the ground. It is the smallest of all seeds, [32] but it becomes the largest of all garden plants; it grows long branches, and birds can make nests in its shade." [33] Jesus used many similar stories and illustrations to teach the people as much as they could understand. [34] In fact, in his public ministry he never taught without using parables; but afterward, when he was alone with his disciples, he explained everything to them.

JESUS CALMS THE STORM

35 As evening came, Jesus said to his disciples, "Let's cross to the other side of the lake." 36 So they took Jesus in the boat and started out, leaving the crowds behind (although other boats followed). 37 But soon a fierce storm came up. High waves were breaking into the boat, and it began to fill with water. 38 Jesus was sleeping at the back of the boat with his head on a cushion. The disciples woke him up, shouting, "Teacher, don't you care that we're going to drown?" 39 When Jesus woke up, he rebuked the wind and said to the waves, "Silence! Be still!" Suddenly the wind stopped, and there was a great calm. 40 Then he asked them, "Why are you afraid? Do you still have no faith?" 41 The disciples were absolutely terrified. "Who is this man?" they asked each other. "Even the wind and waves obey him!"

CHAPTER 4

ALABASTER | GOSPEL OF MARK

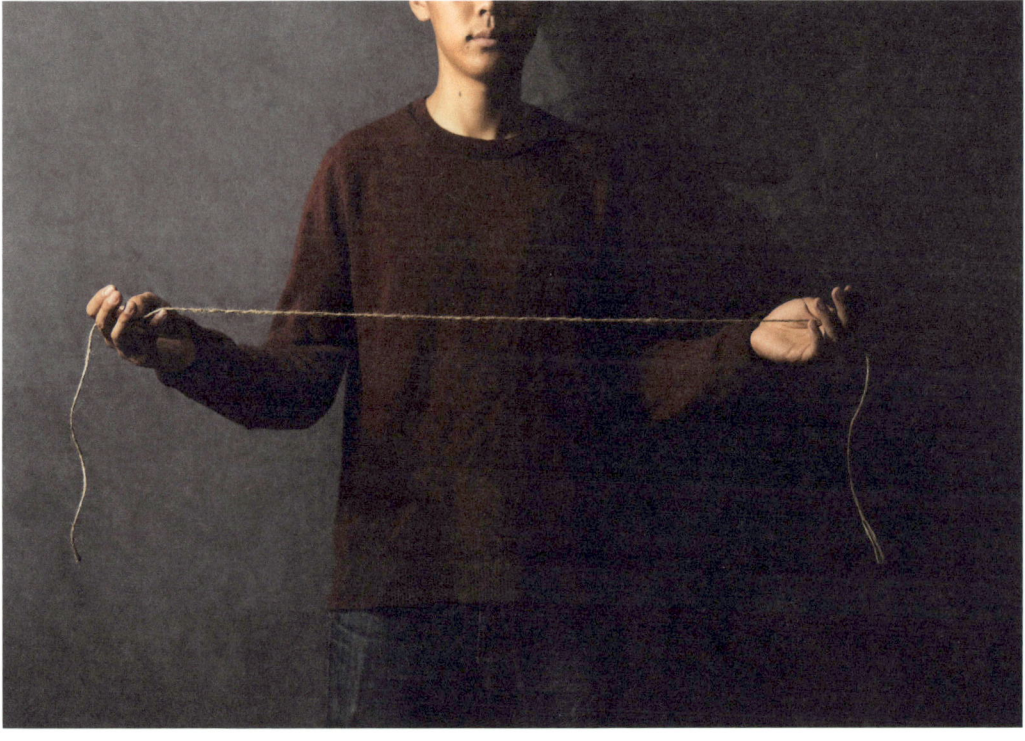

5

JESUS HEALS A DEMON-POSSESSED MAN

[1] So they arrived at the other side of the lake, in the region of the Gerasenes. [2] When Jesus climbed out of the boat, a man possessed by an evil spirit came out from the tombs to meet him. [3] This man lived in the burial caves and could no longer be restrained, even with a chain. [4] Whenever he was put into chains and shackles—as he often was—he snapped the chains from his wrists and smashed the shackles. No one was strong enough to subdue him. [5] Day and night he wandered among the burial caves and in the hills, howling and cutting himself with sharp stones. [6] When Jesus was still some distance away, the man saw him, ran to meet him, and bowed low before him. [7] With a shriek, he screamed, "Why are you interfering with me, Jesus, Son of the Most High God? In the name of God, I beg you, don't torture me!" [8] For Jesus had already said to the spirit, "Come out of the man, you evil spirit." [9] Then Jesus demanded, "What is your name?" And he replied, "My name is Legion, because there are many of us inside this man." [10] Then the evil spirits begged him again and again not to send them to some distant place. [11] There happened to be a large herd of pigs feeding on the hillside nearby. [12] "Send us into those pigs," the spirits begged. "Let us enter them." [13] So Jesus gave them permission. The evil spirits came out of the man and entered the pigs, and the entire herd of about 2,000 pigs plunged down the steep hillside into the lake and drowned in the water. [14] The herdsmen fled to the nearby town and the surrounding countryside, spreading the news as they ran. People rushed out to see what had happened. [15] A crowd soon gathered around Jesus, and they saw the man who had been possessed by the legion of demons. He was sitting there fully clothed and perfectly sane, and they were all afraid. [16] Then those who had seen what happened told the others about the demon-possessed man and the pigs. [17] And the crowd began pleading with Jesus to go away and leave them alone. [18] As Jesus was getting into the boat, the man who had been demon possessed begged to go with him. [19] But Jesus said, "No, go home to your family, and tell them everything the Lord has done for you and how merciful he has been." [20] So the man started off to visit the Ten Towns of that region and began to proclaim the great things Jesus had done for him; and everyone was amazed at what he told them.

JESUS HEALS IN RESPONSE TO FAITH

[21] Jesus got into the boat again and went back to the other side of the lake, where a large crowd gathered around him on the shore. [22] Then a leader of the local synagogue, whose name was Jairus, arrived. When he saw Jesus, he fell at his feet, [23] pleading fervently with him. "My little daughter is dying," he said. "Please come and lay your hands on her; heal her so she can live." [24] Jesus went with him, and all the people followed, crowding around him. [25] A woman in the crowd had suffered for twelve years with constant bleeding. [26] She had suffered a great deal from many doctors, and over the years she had spent everything she had to pay them, but she had gotten no better. In fact, she had gotten worse. [27] She had heard about Jesus, so she came up behind him through the crowd and touched his robe. [28] For she thought to herself, "If I can just touch his robe, I will be healed." [29] Immediately the bleeding stopped, and she could feel in her body that she had been healed of her terrible condition. [30] Jesus realized at once that healing power had gone out from him, so he turned around in the crowd and asked, "Who touched my robe?" [31] His disciples said to him, "Look at this crowd pressing around you. How can you ask, 'Who touched me?'" [32] But he kept on looking around to see who had done it. [33] Then the frightened woman, trembling at the realization of what had happened to her, came and fell to her knees in front of him and told him what she had done. [34] And he said to her, "Daughter, your faith has made you well. Go in peace. Your suffering is over." [35] While he was still speaking to her, messengers arrived from the home of Jairus, the leader of the synagogue. They told him, "Your daughter is dead. There's no use troubling the Teacher now." [36] But Jesus overheard them and said to Jairus, "Don't be afraid. Just have faith." [37] Then Jesus stopped the crowd and wouldn't let anyone go with him except Peter, James, and John (the brother of James). [38] When they came to the home of the synagogue leader, Jesus saw much commotion and weeping and wailing. [39] He went inside and asked, "Why all this commotion and weeping? The child isn't dead; she's only asleep." [40] The crowd laughed at him. But he made them all leave, and he took the girl's father and mother and his three disciples into the room where the girl was lying. [41] Holding her hand, he said to her, "Talitha koum," which means "Little girl, get up!" [42] And the girl, who was twelve years old, immediately stood up and walked around! They were overwhelmed and totally amazed. [43] Jesus gave them strict orders not to tell anyone what had happened, and then he told them to give her something to eat.

CHAPTER 5

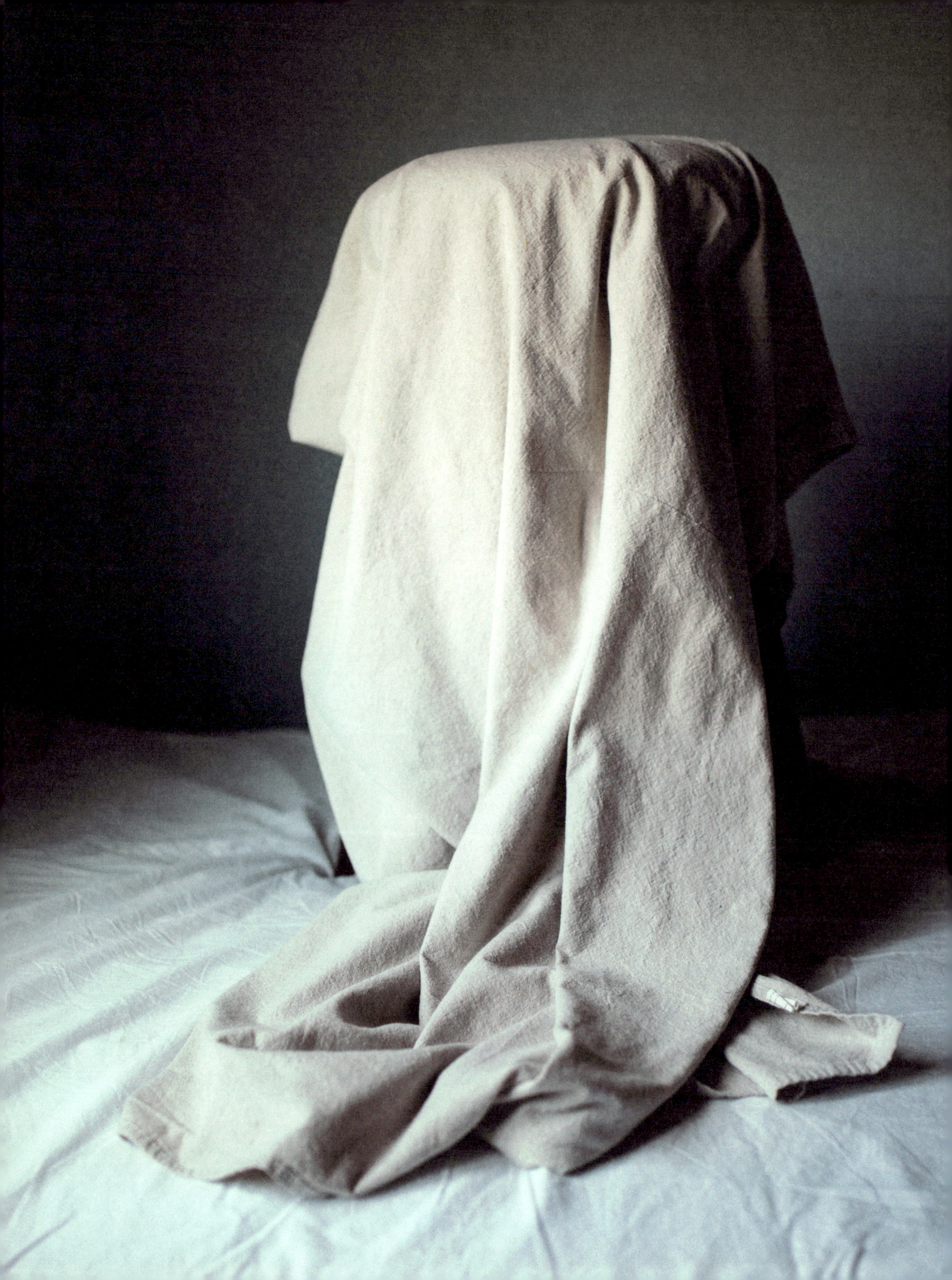

CHAPTER 5

6

CHAPTER 6

JESUS REJECTED AT NAZARETH

[1] Jesus left that part of the country and returned with his disciples to Nazareth, his hometown. [2] The next Sabbath he began teaching in the synagogue, and many who heard him were amazed. They asked, "Where did he get all this wisdom and the power to perform such miracles?" [3] Then they scoffed, "He's just a carpenter, the son of Mary and the brother of James, Joseph, Judas, and Simon. And his sisters live right here among us." They were deeply offended and refused to believe in him. [4] Then Jesus told them, "A prophet is honored everywhere except in his own hometown and among his relatives and his own family." [5] And because of their unbelief, he couldn't do any miracles among them except to place his hands on a few sick people and heal them. [6] And he was amazed at their unbelief.

JESUS SENDS OUT THE TWELVE DISCIPLES

Then Jesus went from village to village, teaching the people. [7] And he called his twelve disciples together and began sending them out two by two, giving them authority to cast out evil spirits. [8] He told them to take nothing for their journey except a walking stick—no food, no traveler's bag, no money. [9] He allowed them to wear sandals but not to take a change of clothes. [10] "Wherever you go," he said, "stay in the same house until you leave town. [11] But if any place refuses to welcome you or listen to you, shake its dust from your feet as you leave to show that you have abandoned those people to their fate." [12] So the disciples went out, telling everyone they met to repent of their sins and turn to God. [13] And they cast out many demons and healed many sick people, anointing them with olive oil.

THE DEATH OF JOHN THE BAPTIST

[14] Herod Antipas, the king, soon heard about Jesus, because everyone was talking about him. Some were saying, "This must be John the Baptist raised from the dead. That is why he can do such miracles." [15] Others said, "He's the prophet Elijah." Still others said, "He's a prophet like the other great prophets of the past." [16] When Herod heard about Jesus, he said, "John, the man I beheaded, has come back from the dead." [17] For Herod had sent soldiers to arrest and imprison John as a favor to Herodias. She had been his brother Philip's wife, but Herod had married her. [18] John had been telling Herod, "It is against God's law for you to marry your brother's wife." [19] So Herodias bore a grudge against John and wanted to kill him. But without Herod's approval she was powerless, [20] for Herod respected John; and knowing that he was a good and holy man, he protected him. Herod was greatly disturbed whenever he talked with John, but even so, he liked to listen to him. [21] Herodias's chance finally came on Herod's birthday. He gave a party for his high government officials, army officers, and the leading citizens of Galilee. [22] Then his daughter, also named Herodias, came in and performed a dance that greatly pleased Herod and his guests. "Ask me for anything you like," the king said to the girl, "and I will give it to you." [23] He even vowed, "I will give you whatever you ask, up to half my kingdom!" [24] She went out and asked her mother, "What should I ask for?" Her mother told her, "Ask for the head of John the Baptist!" [25] So the girl hurried back to the king and told him, "I want the head of John the Baptist, right now, on a tray!" [26] Then the king deeply regretted what he had said; but because of the vows he had made in front of his guests, he couldn't refuse her. [27] So he immediately sent an executioner to the prison to cut off John's head and bring it to him. The soldier beheaded John in the prison, [28] brought his head on a tray, and gave it to the girl, who took it to her mother. [29] When John's disciples heard what had happened, they came to get his body and buried it in a tomb.

ALABASTER | GOSPEL OF MARK

CHAPTER 6

JESUS FEEDS FIVE THOUSAND

[30] The apostles returned to Jesus from their ministry tour and told him all they had done and taught. [31] Then Jesus said, "Let's go off by ourselves to a quiet place and rest awhile." He said this because there were so many people coming and going that Jesus and his apostles didn't even have time to eat. [32] So they left by boat for a quiet place, where they could be alone. [33] But many people recognized them and saw them leaving, and people from many towns ran ahead along the shore and got there ahead of them. [34] Jesus saw the huge crowd as he stepped from the boat, and he had compassion on them because they were like sheep without a shepherd. So he began teaching them many things. [35] Late in the afternoon his disciples came to him and said, "This is a remote place, and it's already getting late. [36] Send the crowds away so they can go to the nearby farms and villages and buy something to eat." [37] But Jesus said, "You feed them." "With what?" they asked. "We'd have to work for months to earn enough money to buy food for all these people!" [38] "How much bread do you have?" he asked. "Go and find out." They came back and reported, "We have five loaves of bread and two fish." [39] Then Jesus told the disciples to have the people sit down in groups on the green grass. [40] So they sat down in groups of fifty or a hundred. [41] Jesus took the five loaves and two fish, looked up toward heaven, and blessed them. Then, breaking the loaves into pieces, he kept giving the bread to the disciples so they could distribute it to the people. He also divided the fish for everyone to share. [42] They all ate as much as they wanted, [43] and afterward, the disciples picked up twelve baskets of leftover bread and fish. [44] A total of 5,000 men and their families were fed.

JESUS WALKS ON WATER

[45] Immediately after this, Jesus insisted that his disciples get back into the boat and head across the lake to Bethsaida, while he sent the people home. [46] After telling everyone good-bye, he went up into the hills by himself to pray. [47] Late that night, the disciples were in their boat in the middle of the lake, and Jesus was alone on land. [48] He saw that they were in serious trouble, rowing hard and struggling against the wind and waves. About three o'clock in the morning Jesus came toward them, walking on the water. He intended to go past them, [49] but when they saw him walking on the water, they cried out in terror, thinking he was a ghost. [50] They were all terrified when they saw him. But Jesus spoke to them at once.

"Don't be afraid," he said. "Take courage! I am here!" ⁵¹ Then he climbed into the boat, and the wind stopped. They were totally amazed, ⁵² for they still didn't understand the significance of the miracle of the loaves. Their hearts were too hard to take it in. ⁵³ After they had crossed the lake, they landed at Gennesaret. They brought the boat to shore ⁵⁴ and climbed out. The people recognized Jesus at once, ⁵⁵ and they ran throughout the whole area, carrying sick people on mats to wherever they heard he was. ⁵⁶ Wherever he went—in villages, cities, or the countryside—they brought the sick out to the marketplaces. They begged him to let the sick touch at least the fringe of his robe, and all who touched him were healed.

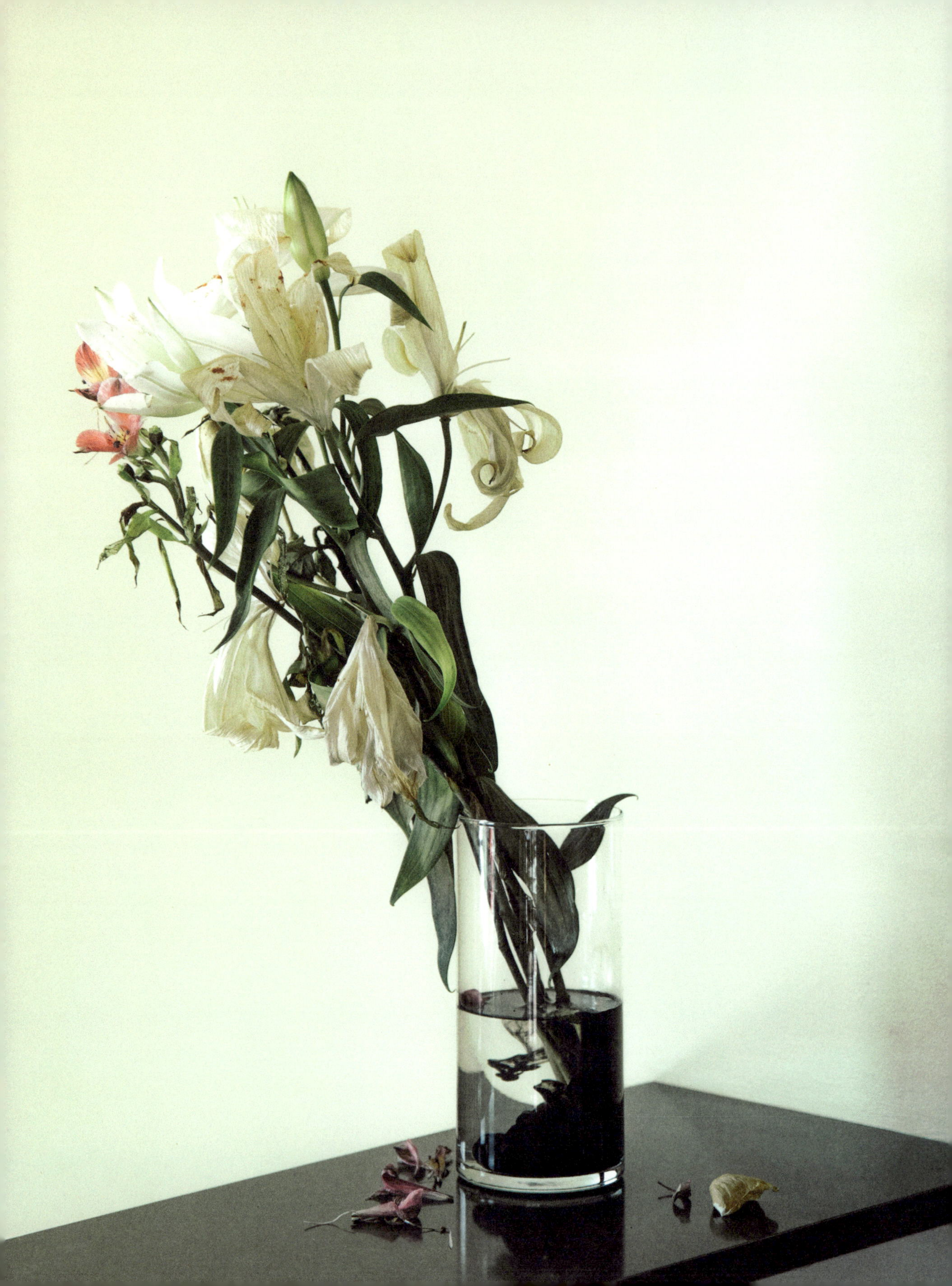

7

JESUS TEACHES ABOUT INNER PURITY

¹ One day some Pharisees and teachers of religious law arrived from Jerusalem to see Jesus. ² They noticed that some of his disciples failed to follow the Jewish ritual of hand washing before eating. ³ (The Jews, especially the Pharisees, do not eat until they have poured water over their cupped hands, as required by their ancient traditions. ⁴ Similarly, they don't eat anything from the market until they immerse their hands in water. This is but one of many traditions they have clung to—such as their ceremonial washing of cups, pitchers, and kettles.) ⁵ So the Pharisees and teachers of religious law asked him, "Why don't your disciples follow our age-old tradition? They eat without first performing the hand-washing ceremony."
⁶ Jesus replied, "You hypocrites! Isaiah was right when he prophesied about you, for he wrote, 'These people honor me with their lips, but their hearts are far from me. ⁷ Their worship is a farce, for they teach man-made ideas as commands from God.' ⁸ For you ignore God's law and substitute your own tradition." ⁹ Then he said, "You skillfully sidestep God's law in order to hold on to your own tradition. ¹⁰ For instance, Moses gave you this law from God: 'Honor your father and mother,' and 'Anyone who speaks disrespectfully of father or mother must be put to death.' ¹¹ But you say it is all right for people to say to their parents, 'Sorry, I can't help you. For I have vowed to give to God what I would have given to you.'¹² In this way, you let them disregard their needy parents. ¹³ And so you cancel the word of God in order to hand down your own tradition. And this is only one example among many others." ¹⁴ Then Jesus called to the crowd to come and hear. "All of you listen," he said, "and try to understand. ¹⁵ It's not what goes into your body that defiles you; you are defiled by what comes from your heart." ¹⁷ Then Jesus went into a house to get away from the crowd, and his disciples asked him what he meant by the parable he had just used. ¹⁸ "Don't you understand either?" he asked. "Can't you see that the food you put into your body cannot defile you? ¹⁹ Food doesn't go into your heart, but only passes through the stomach and then goes into the sewer." (By saying this, he declared that every kind of food is acceptable in God's eyes.) ²⁰ And then he added, "It is what comes from inside that defiles you. ²¹ For from within, out of a person's heart, come evil thoughts, sexual immorality, theft, murder, ²² adultery, greed, wickedness, deceit, lustful desires, envy, slander, pride, and foolishness. ²³ All these vile things come from within; they are what defile you."

THE FAITH OF A GENTILE WOMAN

[24] Then Jesus left Galilee and went north to the region of Tyre. He didn't want anyone to know which house he was staying in, but he couldn't keep it a secret. [25] Right away a woman who had heard about him came and fell at his feet. Her little girl was possessed by an evil spirit, [26] and she begged him to cast out the demon from her daughter. Since she was a Gentile, born in Syrian Phoenicia, [27] Jesus told her, "First I should feed the children—my own family, the Jews. It isn't right to take food from the children and throw it to the dogs." [28] She replied, "That's true, Lord, but even the dogs under the table are allowed to eat the scraps from the children's plates." [29] "Good answer!" he said. "Now go home, for the demon has left your daughter." [30] And when she arrived home, she found her little girl lying quietly in bed, and the demon was gone.

JESUS HEALS A DEAF MAN

[31] Jesus left Tyre and went up to Sidon before going back to the Sea of Galilee and the region of the Ten Towns. [32] A deaf man with a speech impediment was brought to him, and the people begged Jesus to lay his hands on the man to heal him. [33] Jesus led him away from the crowd so they could be alone. He put his fingers into the man's ears. Then, spitting on his own fingers, he touched the man's tongue. [34] Looking up to heaven, he sighed and said, "Ephphatha," which means, "Be opened!" [35] Instantly the man could hear perfectly, and his tongue was freed so he could speak plainly! [36] Jesus told the crowd not to tell anyone, but the more he told them not to, the more they spread the news. [37] They were completely amazed and said again and again, "Everything he does is wonderful. He even makes the deaf to hear and gives speech to those who cannot speak."

CHAPTER 7

ALABASTER | GOSPEL OF MARK

8

JESUS FEEDS FOUR THOUSAND

¹ About this time another large crowd had gathered, and the people ran out of food again. Jesus called his disciples and told them, ² "I feel sorry for these people. They have been here with me for three days, and they have nothing left to eat. ³ If I send them home hungry, they will faint along the way. For some of them have come a long distance." ⁴ His disciples replied, "How are we supposed to find enough food to feed them out here in the wilderness?" ⁵ Jesus asked, "How much bread do you have?" "Seven loaves," they replied. ⁶ So Jesus told all the people to sit down on the ground. Then he took the seven loaves, thanked God for them, and broke them into pieces. He gave them to his disciples, who distributed the bread to the crowd. ⁷ A few small fish were found, too, so Jesus also blessed these and told the disciples to distribute them. ⁸ They ate as much as they wanted. Afterward, the disciples picked up seven large baskets of leftover food. ⁹ There were about 4,000 men in the crowd that day, and Jesus sent them home after they had eaten. ¹⁰ Immediately after this, he got into a boat with his disciples and crossed over to the region of Dalmanutha.

PHARISEES DEMAND A MIRACULOUS SIGN

¹¹ When the Pharisees heard that Jesus had arrived, they came and started to argue with him. Testing him, they demanded that he show them a miraculous sign from heaven to prove his authority. ¹² When he heard this, he sighed deeply in his spirit and said, "Why do these people keep demanding a miraculous sign? I tell you the truth, I will not give this generation any such sign." ¹³ So he got back into the boat and left them, and he crossed to the other side of the lake.

YEAST OF THE PHARISEES AND HEROD

¹⁴ But the disciples had forgotten to bring any food. They had only one loaf of bread with them in the boat. ¹⁵ As they were crossing the lake, Jesus warned them, "Watch out! Beware of the yeast of the Pharisees and of Herod." ¹⁶ At this they began to argue with each other because they hadn't brought any bread. ¹⁷ Jesus knew what they were saying, so he said, "Why are you arguing about having no bread? Don't you know or understand even yet? Are your hearts too hard to take it in? ¹⁸ 'You have eyes—can't you see? You have ears—can't you hear?' Don't you remember anything at all? ¹⁹ When I fed the 5,000 with five loaves of bread, how many baskets of leftovers did you pick up afterward?" "Twelve," they said. ²⁰ "And when I fed the 4,000 with seven loaves, how many large baskets of leftovers did you pick up?" "Seven," they said. ²¹ "Don't you understand yet?" he asked them.

JESUS HEALS A BLIND MAN

[22] When they arrived at Bethsaida, some people brought a blind man to Jesus, and they begged him to touch the man and heal him. [23] Jesus took the blind man by the hand and led him out of the village. Then, spitting on the man's eyes, he laid his hands on him and asked, "Can you see anything now?" [24] The man looked around. "Yes," he said, "I see people, but I can't see them very clearly. They look like trees walking around." [25] Then Jesus placed his hands on the man's eyes again, and his eyes were opened. His sight was completely restored, and he could see everything clearly. [26] Jesus sent him away, saying, "Don't go back into the village on your way home."

PETER'S DECLARATION ABOUT JESUS

[27] Jesus and his disciples left Galilee and went up to the villages near Caesarea Philippi. As they were walking along, he asked them, "Who do people say I am?" [28] "Well," they replied, "some say John the Baptist, some say Elijah, and others say you are one of the other prophets." [29] Then he asked them, "But who do you say I am?" Peter replied, "You are the Messiah." [30] But Jesus warned them not to tell anyone about him.

CHAPTER 8

JESUS PREDICTS HIS DEATH

[31] Then Jesus began to tell them that the Son of Man must suffer many terrible things and be rejected by the elders, the leading priests, and the teachers of religious law. He would be killed, but three days later he would rise from the dead. [32] As he talked about this openly with his disciples, Peter took him aside and began to reprimand him for saying such things. [33] Jesus turned around and looked at his disciples, then reprimanded Peter. "Get away from me, Satan!" he said. "You are seeing things merely from a human point of view, not from God's." [34] Then, calling the crowd to join his disciples, he said, "If any of you wants to be my follower, you must give up your own way, take up your cross, and follow me. [35] If you try to hang on to your life, you will lose it. But if you give up your life for my sake and for the sake of the Good News, you will save it. [36] And what do you benefit if you gain the whole world but lose your own soul? [37] Is anything worth more than your soul? [38] If anyone is ashamed of me and my message in these adulterous and sinful days, the Son of Man will be ashamed of that person when he returns in the glory of his Father with the holy angels."

CHAPTER 8

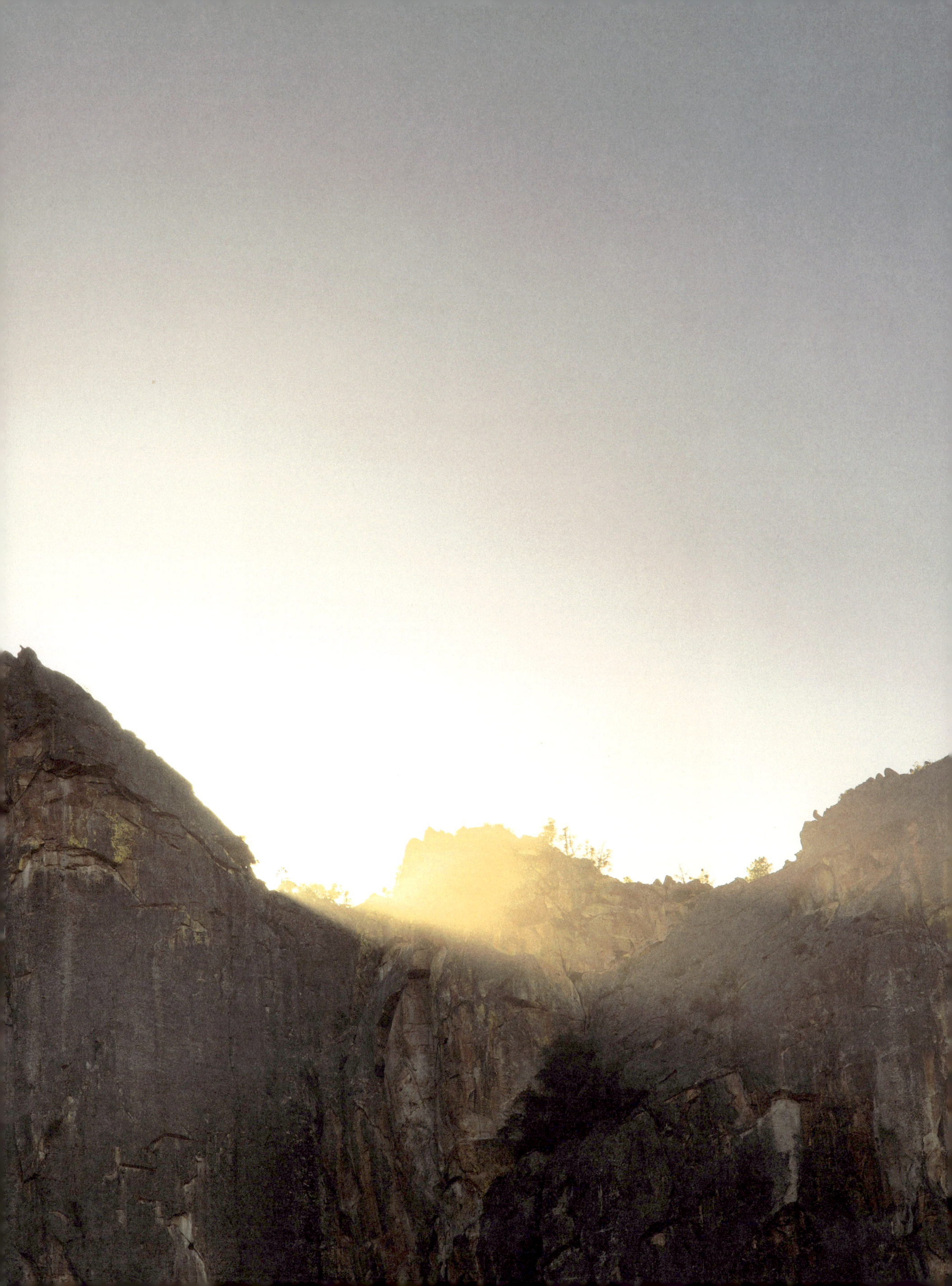

9

[1] Jesus went on to say, "I tell you the truth, some standing here right now will not die before they see the Kingdom of God arrive in great power!"

THE TRANSFIGURATION

[2] Six days later Jesus took Peter, James, and John, and led them up a high mountain to be alone. As the men watched, Jesus' appearance was transformed, [3] and his clothes became dazzling white, far whiter than any earthly bleach could ever make them. [4] Then Elijah and Moses appeared and began talking with Jesus. [5] Peter exclaimed, "Rabbi, it's wonderful for us to be here! Let's make three shelters as memorials—one for you, one for Moses, and one for Elijah." [6] He said this because he didn't really know what else to say, for they were all terrified. [7] Then a cloud overshadowed them, and a voice from the cloud said, "This is my dearly loved Son. Listen to him." [8] Suddenly, when they looked around, Moses and Elijah were gone, and they saw only Jesus with them. [9] As they went back down the mountain, he told them not to tell anyone what they had seen until the Son of Man had risen from the dead. [10] So they kept it to themselves, but they often asked each other what he meant by "rising from the dead." [11] Then they asked him, "Why do the teachers of religious law insist that Elijah must return before the Messiah comes?" [12] Jesus responded, "Elijah is indeed coming first to get everything ready. Yet why do the Scriptures say that the Son of Man must suffer greatly and be treated with utter contempt? [13] But I tell you, Elijah has already come, and they chose to abuse him, just as the Scriptures predicted."

JESUS HEALS A DEMON-POSSESSED BOY

[14] When they returned to the other disciples, they saw a large crowd surrounding them, and some teachers of religious law were arguing with them. [15] When the crowd saw Jesus, they were overwhelmed with awe, and they ran to greet him. [16] "What is all this arguing about?" Jesus asked. [17] One of the men in the crowd spoke up and said, "Teacher, I brought my son so you could heal him. He is possessed by an evil spirit that won't let him talk. [18] And whenever this spirit seizes him, it throws him violently to the ground. Then he foams at the mouth and grinds his teeth and becomes rigid. So I asked your disciples to cast out the evil spirit, but they couldn't do it." [19] Jesus said to them, "You faithless people! How long must I be with you? How long must I put up with you? Bring the boy to me." [20] So they brought the boy. But when the evil spirit saw Jesus, it threw the child into a violent convulsion, and he fell to the ground, writhing and foaming at the mouth. [21] "How long has this been happening?" Jesus asked the boy's father. He replied, "Since he was a little boy. [22] The spirit often throws him into the fire or into water, trying to kill him. Have mercy on us and help us, if you can." [23] "What do you mean, 'If I can'?" Jesus asked. "Anything is possible if a person believes." [24] The father instantly cried out, "I do believe, but help me overcome my unbelief!" [25] When Jesus saw that the crowd of onlookers was growing, he rebuked the evil spirit. "Listen, you spirit that makes this boy unable to hear and speak," he said. "I command you to come out of this child and never enter him again!" [26] Then the spirit screamed and threw the boy into another violent convulsion and left him. The boy appeared to be dead. A murmur ran through the crowd as people said, "He's dead." [27] But Jesus took him by the hand and helped him to his feet, and he stood up. [28] Afterward, when Jesus was alone in the house with his disciples, they asked him, "Why couldn't we cast out that evil spirit?" [29] Jesus replied, "This kind can be cast out only by prayer."

JESUS AGAIN PREDICTS HIS DEATH

[30] Leaving that region, they traveled through Galilee. Jesus didn't want anyone to know he was there, [31] for he wanted to spend more time with his disciples and teach them. He said to them, "The Son of Man is going to be betrayed into the hands of his enemies. He will be killed, but three days later he will rise from the dead." [32] They didn't understand what he was saying, however, and they were afraid to ask him what he meant.

CHAPTER 9

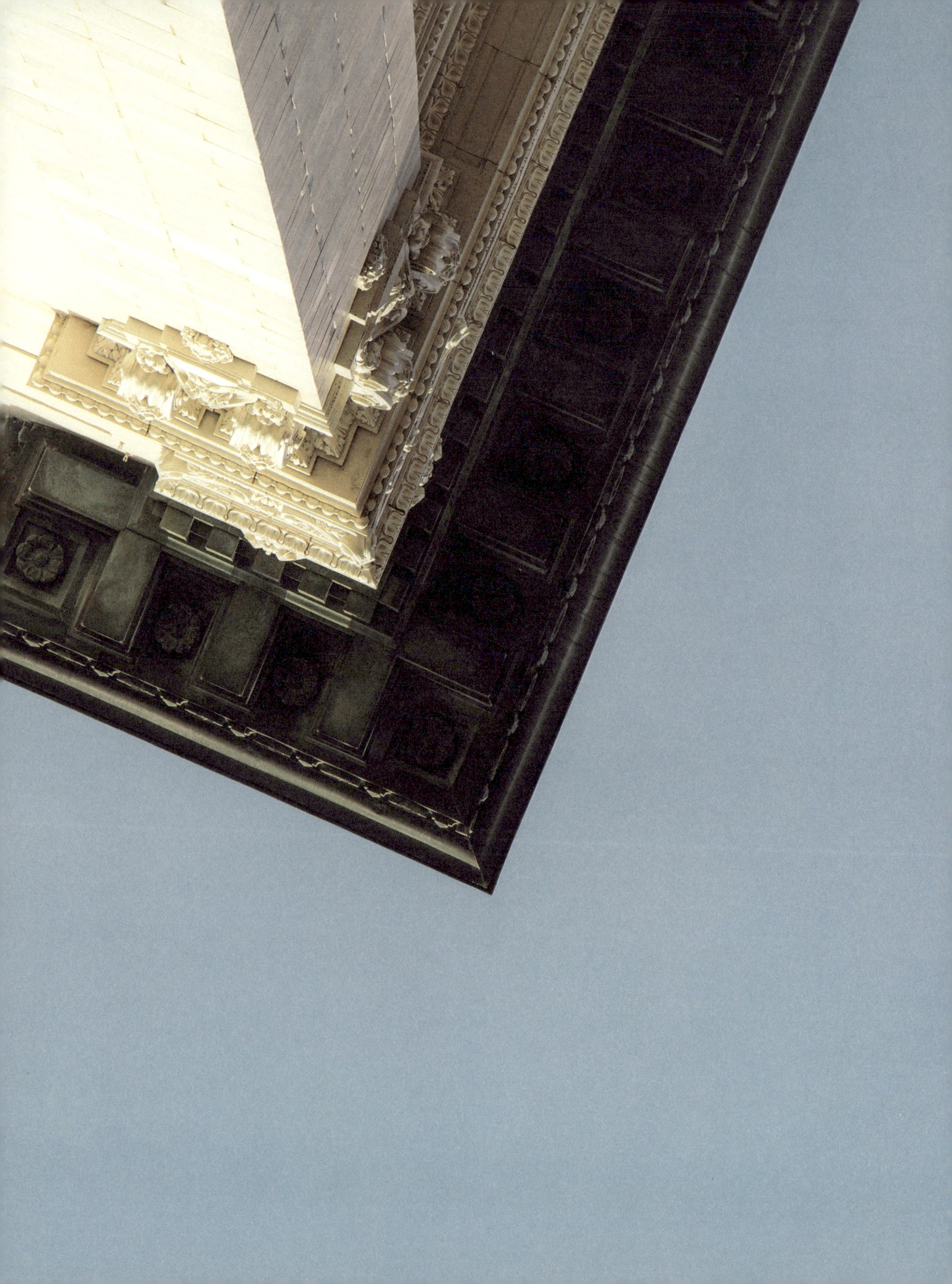

THE GREATEST IN THE KINGDOM

³³ After they arrived at Capernaum and settled in a house, Jesus asked his disciples, "What were you discussing out on the road?" ³⁴ But they didn't answer, because they had been arguing about which of them was the greatest. ³⁵ He sat down, called the twelve disciples over to him, and said, "Whoever wants to be first must take last place and be the servant of everyone else." ³⁶ Then he put a little child among them. Taking the child in his arms, he said to them, ³⁷ "Anyone who welcomes a little child like this on my behalf welcomes me, and anyone who welcomes me welcomes not only me but also my Father who sent me."

USING THE NAME OF JESUS

[38] John said to Jesus, "Teacher, we saw someone using your name to cast out demons, but we told him to stop because he wasn't in our group." [39] "Don't stop him!" Jesus said. "No one who performs a miracle in my name will soon be able to speak evil of me. [40] Anyone who is not against us is for us. [41] If anyone gives you even a cup of water because you belong to the Messiah, I tell you the truth, that person will surely be rewarded. [42] "But if you cause one of these little ones who trusts in me to fall into sin, it would be better for you to be thrown into the sea with a large millstone hung around your neck. [43] If your hand causes you to sin, cut it off. It's better to enter eternal life with only one hand than to go into the unquenchable fires of hell with two hands. [45] If your foot causes you to sin, cut it off. It's better to enter eternal life with only one foot than to be thrown into hell with two feet. [47] And if your eye causes you to sin, gouge it out. It's better to enter the Kingdom of God with only one eye than to have two eyes and be thrown into hell, [48] 'where the maggots never die and the fire never goes out.' [49] "For everyone will be tested with fire. [50] Salt is good for seasoning. But if it loses its flavor, how do you make it salty again? You must have the qualities of salt among yourselves and live in peace with each other."

CHAPTER 9

ALABASTER | GOSPEL OF MARK

10

¹ Then Jesus left Capernaum and went down to the region of Judea and into the area east of the Jordan River. Once again crowds gathered around him, and as usual he was teaching them. ² Some Pharisees came and tried to trap him with this question: "Should a man be allowed to divorce his wife?" ³ Jesus answered them with a question: "What did Moses say in the law about divorce?" ⁴ "Well, he permitted it," they replied. "He said a man can give his wife a written notice of divorce and send her away." ⁵ But Jesus responded, "He wrote this commandment only as a concession to your hard hearts. ⁶ But 'God made them male and female' from the beginning of creation. ⁷ 'This explains why a man leaves his father and mother and is joined to his wife, ⁸ and the two are united into one.' Since they are no longer two but one, ⁹ let no one split apart what God has joined together." ¹⁰ Later, when he was alone with his disciples in the house, they brought up the subject again. ¹¹ He told them, "Whoever divorces his wife and marries someone else commits adultery against her. ¹² And if a woman divorces her husband and marries someone else, she commits adultery."

JESUS BLESSES THE CHILDREN

¹³ One day some parents brought their children to Jesus so he could touch and bless them. But the disciples scolded the parents for bothering him. ¹⁴ When Jesus saw what was happening, he was angry with his disciples. He said to them, "Let the children come to me. Don't stop them! For the Kingdom of God belongs to those who are like these children. ¹⁵ I tell you the truth, anyone who doesn't receive the Kingdom of God like a child will never enter it." ¹⁶ Then he took the children in his arms and placed his hands on their heads and blessed them.

THE RICH MAN

[17] As Jesus was starting out on his way to Jerusalem, a man came running up to him, knelt down, and asked, "Good Teacher, what must I do to inherit eternal life?" [18] "Why do you call me good?" Jesus asked. "Only God is truly good. [19] But to answer your question, you know the commandments: 'You must not murder. You must not commit adultery. You must not steal. You must not testify falsely. You must not cheat anyone. Honor your father and mother.'" [20] "Teacher," the man replied, "I've obeyed all these commandments since I was young." [21] Looking at the man, Jesus felt genuine love for him. "There is still one thing you haven't done," he told him. "Go and sell all your possessions and give the money to the poor, and you will have treasure in heaven. Then come, follow me." [22] At this the man's face fell, and he went away sad, for he had many possessions. [23] Jesus looked around and said to his disciples, "How hard it is for the rich to enter the Kingdom of God!" [24] This amazed them. But Jesus said again, "Dear children, it is very hard to enter the Kingdom of God. [25] In fact, it is easier for a camel to go through the eye of a needle than for a rich person to enter the Kingdom of God!" [26] The

CHAPTER 10

disciples were astounded. "Then who in the world can be saved?" they asked. [27] Jesus looked at them intently and said, "Humanly speaking, it is impossible. But not with God. Everything is possible with God." [28] Then Peter began to speak up. "We've given up everything to follow you," he said. [29] "Yes," Jesus replied, "and I assure you that everyone who has given up house or brothers or sisters or mother or father or children or property, for my sake and for the Good News, [30] will receive now in return a hundred times as many houses, brothers, sisters, mothers, children, and property—along with persecution. And in the world to come that person will have eternal life. [31] But many who are the greatest now will be least important then, and those who seem least important now will be the greatest then."

ALABASTER | GOSPEL OF MARK

JESUS AGAIN PREDICTS HIS DEATH

[32] They were now on the way up to Jerusalem, and Jesus was walking ahead of them. The disciples were filled with awe, and the people following behind were overwhelmed with fear. Taking the twelve disciples aside, Jesus once more began to describe everything that was about to happen to him. [33] "Listen," he said, "we're going up to Jerusalem, where the Son of Man will be betrayed to the leading priests and the teachers of religious law. They will sentence him to die and hand him over to the Romans. [34] They will mock him, spit on him, flog him with a whip, and kill him, but after three days he will rise again."

JESUS TEACHES ABOUT SERVING OTHERS

[35] Then James and John, the sons of Zebedee, came over and spoke to him. "Teacher," they said, "we want you to do us a favor." [36] "What is your request?" he asked. [37] They replied, "When you sit on your glorious throne, we want to sit in places of honor next to you, one on your right and the other on your left." [38] But Jesus said to them, "You don't know what you are asking! Are you able to drink from the bitter cup of suffering I am about to drink? Are you able to be baptized with the baptism of suffering I must be baptized with?" [39] "Oh yes," they replied, "we are able!" Then Jesus told them, "You will indeed drink from my bitter cup and be baptized with my baptism of suffering. [40] But I have no right to say who will sit on my right or my left. God has prepared those places for the ones he has chosen." [41] When the ten other disciples heard what James and John had asked, they were indignant. [42] So Jesus called them together and said, "You know that the rulers in this world lord it over their people, and officials flaunt their authority over those under them. [43] But among you it will be different. Whoever wants to be a leader among you must be your servant, [44] and whoever wants to be first among you must be the slave of everyone else. [45] For even the Son of Man came not to be served but to serve others and to give his life as a ransom for many."

JESUS HEALS BLIND BARTIMAEUS

[46] Then they reached Jericho, and as Jesus and his disciples left town, a large crowd followed him. A blind beggar named Bartimaeus (son of Timaeus) was sitting beside the road. [47] When Bartimaeus heard that Jesus of Nazareth was nearby, he began to shout, "Jesus, Son of David, have mercy on me!" [48] "Be quiet!" many of the people yelled at him. But he only shouted louder, "Son of David, have mercy on me!" [49] When Jesus heard him, he stopped and said, "Tell him to come here." So they called the blind man. "Cheer up," they said. "Come on, he's calling you!" [50] Bartimaeus threw aside his coat, jumped up, and came to Jesus. [51] "What do you want me to do for you?" Jesus asked. "My Rabbi," the blind man said, "I want to see!" [52] And Jesus said to him, "Go, for your faith has healed you." Instantly the man could see, and he followed Jesus down the road.

11

JESUS' TRIUMPHANT ENTRY

¹ As Jesus and his disciples approached Jerusalem, they came to the towns of Bethphage and Bethany on the Mount of Olives. Jesus sent two of them on ahead. ² "Go into that village over there," he told them. "As soon as you enter it, you will see a young donkey tied there that no one has ever ridden. Untie it and bring it here. ³ If anyone asks, 'What are you doing?' just say, 'The Lord needs it and will return it soon.'" ⁴ The two disciples left and found the colt standing in the street, tied outside the front door. ⁵ As they were untying it, some bystanders demanded, "What are you doing, untying that colt?" ⁶ They said what Jesus had told them to say, and they were permitted to take it. ⁷ Then they brought the colt to Jesus and threw their garments over it, and he sat on it. ⁸ Many in the crowd spread their garments on the road ahead of him, and others spread leafy branches they had cut in the fields. ⁹ Jesus was in the center of the procession, and the people all around him were shouting, "Praise God! Blessings on the one who comes in the name of the Lord! ¹⁰ Blessings on the coming Kingdom of our ancestor David! Praise God in highest heaven!" ¹¹ So Jesus came to Jerusalem and went into the Temple. After looking around carefully at everything, he left because it was late in the afternoon. Then he returned to Bethany with the twelve disciples.

ALABASTER | GOSPEL OF MARK

CHAPTER 11

JESUS CURSES THE FIG TREE

[12] The next morning as they were leaving Bethany, Jesus was hungry. [13] He noticed a fig tree in full leaf a little way off, so he went over to see if he could find any figs. But there were only leaves because it was too early in the season for fruit. [14] Then Jesus said to the tree, "May no one ever eat your fruit again!" And the disciples heard him say it.

JESUS CLEARS THE TEMPLE

[15] When they arrived back in Jerusalem, Jesus entered the Temple and began to drive out the people buying and selling animals for sacrifices. He knocked over the tables of the money changers and the chairs of those selling doves, [16] and he stopped everyone from using the Temple as a marketplace. [17] He said to them, "The Scriptures declare, 'My Temple will be called a house of prayer for all nations,' but you have turned it into a den of thieves." [18] When the leading priests and teachers of religious law heard what Jesus had done, they began planning how to kill him. But they were afraid of him because the people were so amazed at his teaching. [19] That evening Jesus and the disciples left the city. [20] The next morning as they passed by the fig tree he had cursed, the disciples noticed it had withered from the roots up. [21] Peter remembered what Jesus had said to the tree on the previous day and exclaimed, "Look, Rabbi! The fig tree you cursed has withered and died!" [22] Then Jesus said to the disciples, "Have faith in God. [23] I tell you the truth, you can say to this mountain, 'May you be lifted up and thrown into the sea,' and it will happen. But you must really believe it will happen and have no doubt in your heart. [24] I tell you, you can pray for anything, and if you believe that you've received it, it will be yours. [25] But when you are praying, first forgive anyone you are holding a grudge against, so that your Father in heaven will forgive your sins, too."

THE AUTHORITY OF JESUS CHALLENGED

[27] Again they entered Jerusalem. As Jesus was walking through the Temple area, the leading priests, the teachers of religious law, and the elders came up to him. [28] They demanded, "By what authority are you doing all these things? Who gave you the right to do them?" [29] "I'll tell you by what authority I do these things if you answer one question," Jesus replied. [30] "Did John's authority to baptize come from heaven, or was it merely human? Answer me!" [31] They talked it over among themselves. "If we say it was from heaven, he will ask why we didn't believe John. [32] But do we dare say it was merely human?" For they were afraid of what the people would do, because everyone believed that John was a prophet. [33] So they finally replied, "We don't know." And Jesus responded, "Then I won't tell you by what authority I do these things."

CHAPTER 11

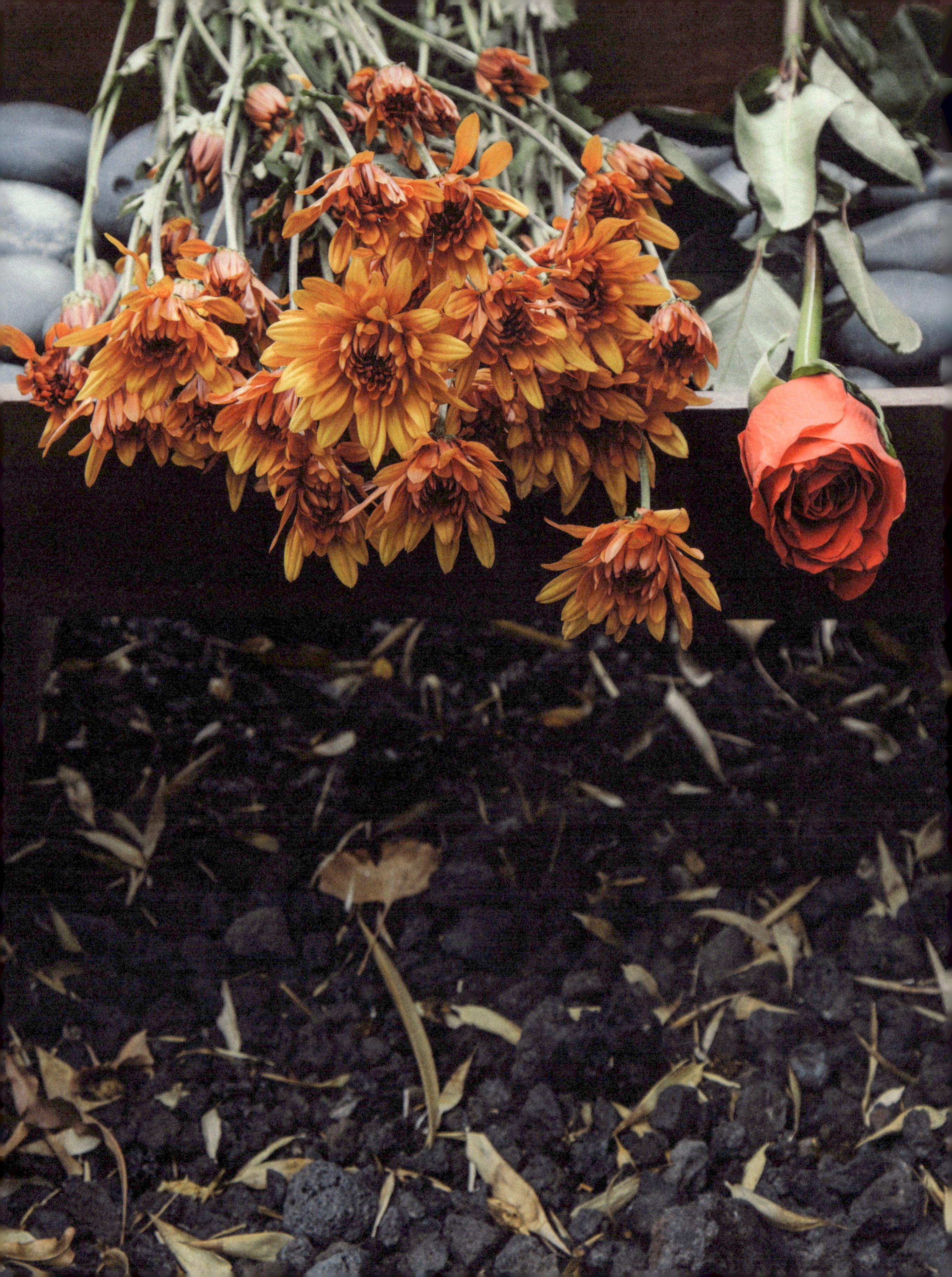

12

PARABLE OF THE EVIL FARMERS

[1] Then Jesus began teaching them with stories: "A man planted a vineyard. He built a wall around it, dug a pit for pressing out the grape juice, and built a lookout tower. Then he leased the vineyard to tenant farmers and moved to another country. [2] At the time of the grape harvest, he sent one of his servants to collect his share of the crop. [3] But the farmers grabbed the servant, beat him up, and sent him back empty-handed. [4] The owner then sent another servant, but they insulted him and beat him over the head. [5] The next servant he sent was killed. Others he sent were either beaten or killed, [6] until there was only one left—his son whom he loved dearly. The owner finally sent him, thinking, 'Surely they will respect my son.' [7] "But the tenant farmers said to one another, 'Here comes the heir to this estate. Let's kill him and get the estate for ourselves!' [8] So they grabbed him and murdered him and threw his body out of the vineyard. [9] "What do you suppose the owner of the vineyard will do?" Jesus asked. "I'll tell you—he will come and kill those farmers and lease the vineyard to others. [10] Didn't you ever read this in the Scriptures? 'The stone that the builders rejected has now become the cornerstone. [11] This is the Lord's doing, and it is wonderful to see.'" [12] The religious leaders wanted to arrest Jesus because they realized he was telling the story against them—they were the wicked farmers. But they were afraid of the crowd, so they left him and went away.

TAXES FOR CAESAR

[13] Later the leaders sent some Pharisees and supporters of Herod to trap Jesus into saying something for which he could be arrested. [14] "Teacher," they said, "we know how honest you are. You are impartial and don't play favorites. You teach the way of God truthfully. Now tell us—is it right to pay taxes to Caesar or not? [15] Should we pay them, or shouldn't we?" Jesus saw through their hypocrisy and said, "Why are you trying to trap me? Show me a Roman coin, and I'll tell you." [16] When they handed it to him, he asked, "Whose picture and title are stamped on it?" "Caesar's," they replied. [17] "Well, then," Jesus said, "give to Caesar what belongs to Caesar, and give to God what belongs to God." His reply completely amazed them.

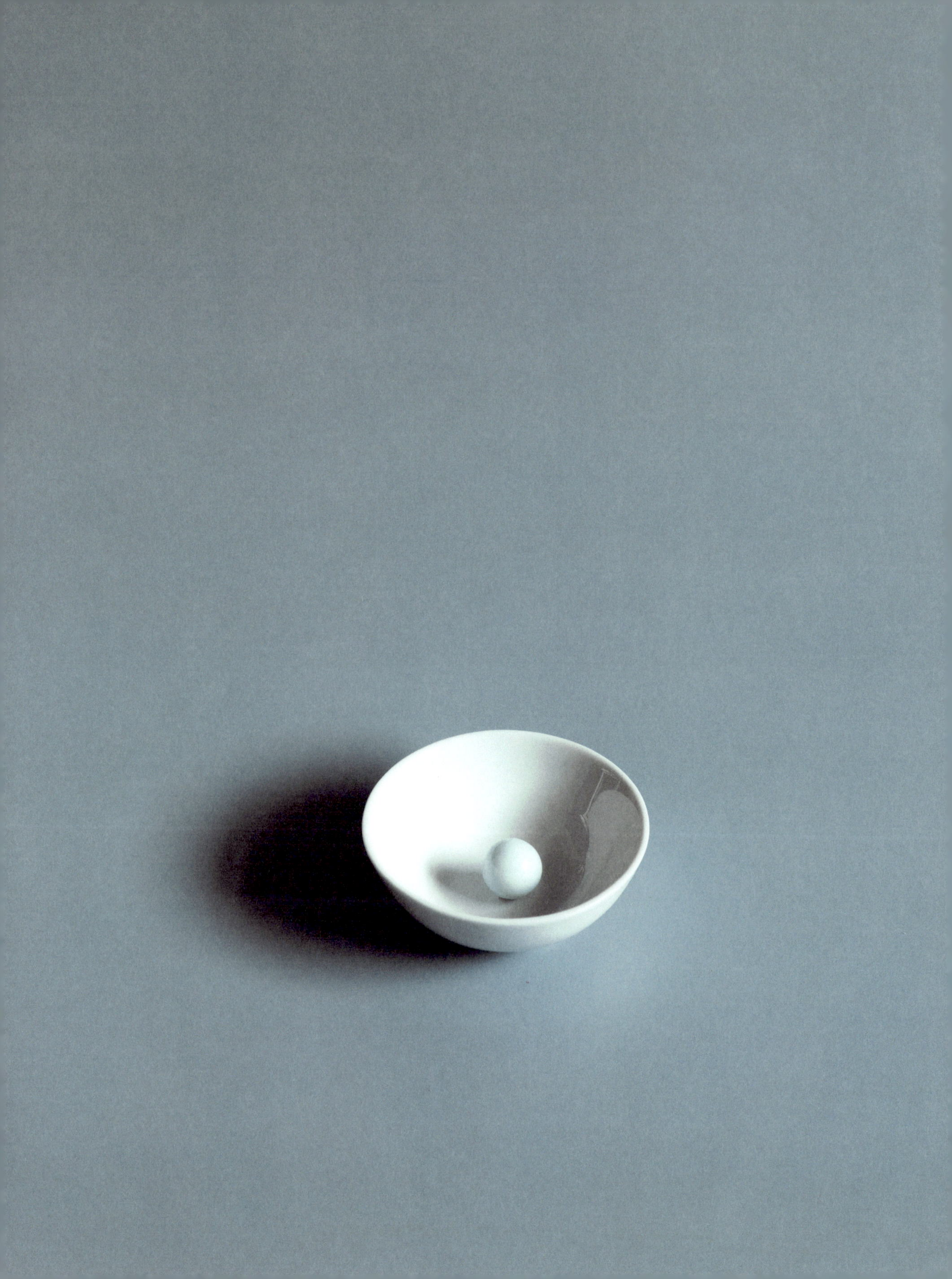

DISCUSSION ABOUT RESURRECTION

[18] Then Jesus was approached by some Sadducees—religious leaders who say there is no resurrection from the dead. They posed this question: [19] "Teacher, Moses gave us a law that if a man dies, leaving a wife without children, his brother should marry the widow and have a child who will carry on the brother's name. [20] Well, suppose there were seven brothers. The oldest one married and then died without children. [21] So the second brother married the widow, but he also died without children. Then the third brother married her. [22] This continued with all seven of them, and still there were no children. Last of all, the woman also died. [23] So tell us, whose wife will she be in the resurrection? For all seven were married to her." [24] Jesus replied, "Your mistake is that you don't know the Scriptures, and you don't know the power of God. [25] For when the dead rise, they will neither marry nor be given in marriage. In this respect they will be like the angels in heaven. [26] "But now, as to whether the dead will be raised—haven't you ever read about this in the writings of Moses, in the story of the burning bush? Long after Abraham, Isaac, and Jacob had died, God said to Moses, 'I am the God of Abraham, the God of Isaac, and the God of Jacob.' [27] So he is the God of the living, not the dead. You have made a serious error."

THE MOST IMPORTANT COMMANDMENT

[28] One of the teachers of religious law was standing there listening to the debate. He realized that Jesus had answered well, so he asked, "Of all the commandments, which is the most important?" [29] Jesus replied, "The most important commandment is this: 'Listen, O Israel! The Lord our God is the one and only Lord. [30] And you must love the Lord your God with all your heart, all your soul, all your mind, and all your strength.' [31] The second is equally important: 'Love your neighbor as yourself.' No other commandment is greater than these." [32] The teacher of religious law replied, "Well said, Teacher. You have spoken the truth by saying that there is only one God and no other. [33] And I know it is important to love him with all my heart and all my understanding and all my strength, and to love my neighbor as myself. This is more important than to offer all of the burnt offerings and sacrifices required in the law." [34] Realizing how much the man understood, Jesus said to him, "You are not far from the Kingdom of God." And after that, no one dared to ask him any more questions.

WHOSE SON IS THE MESSIAH?

[35] Later, as Jesus was teaching the people in the Temple, he asked, "Why do the teachers of religious law claim that the Messiah is the son of David? [36] For David himself, speaking under the inspiration of the Holy Spirit, said, 'The Lord said to my Lord, Sit in the place of honor at my right hand until I humble your enemies beneath your feet.' [37] Since David himself called the Messiah 'my Lord,' how can the Messiah be his son?" The large crowd listened to him with great delight. [38] Jesus also taught: "Beware of these teachers of religious law! For they like to parade around in flowing robes and receive respectful greetings as they walk in the marketplaces. [39] And how they love the seats of honor in the synagogues and the head table at banquets. [40] Yet they shamelessly cheat widows out of their property and then pretend to be pious by making long prayers in public. Because of this, they will be more severely punished."

THE WIDOW'S OFFERING

[41] Jesus sat down near the collection box in the Temple and watched as the crowds dropped in their money. Many rich people put in large amounts. [42] Then a poor widow came and dropped in two small coins. [43] Jesus called his disciples to him and said, "I tell you the truth, this poor widow has given more than all the others who are making contributions. [44] For they gave a tiny part of their surplus, but she, poor as she is, has given everything she had to live on."

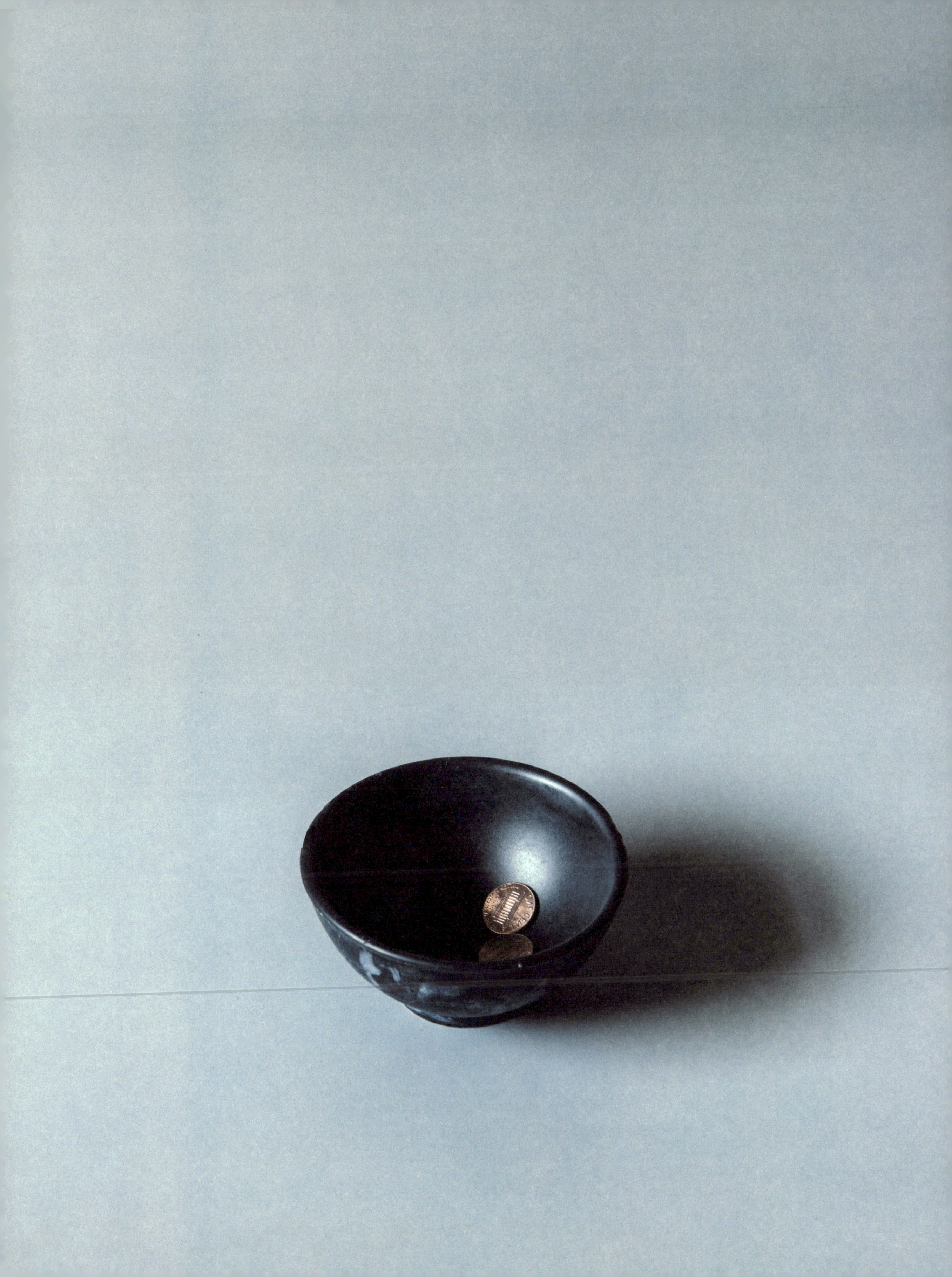

13

JESUS SPEAKS ABOUT THE FUTURE

[1] As Jesus was leaving the Temple that day, one of his disciples said, "Teacher, look at these magnificent buildings! Look at the impressive stones in the walls." [2] Jesus replied, "Yes, look at these great buildings. But they will be completely demolished. Not one stone will be left on top of another!" [3] Later, Jesus sat on the Mount of Olives across the valley from the Temple. Peter, James, John, and Andrew came to him privately and asked him, [4] "Tell us, when will all this happen? What sign will show us that these things are about to be fulfilled?" [5] Jesus replied, "Don't let anyone mislead you, [6] for many will come in my name, claiming, 'I am the Messiah.' They will deceive many. [7] And you

CHAPTER 13

will hear of wars and threats of wars, but don't panic. Yes, these things must take place, but the end won't follow immediately. [8] Nation will go to war against nation, and kingdom against kingdom. There will be earthquakes in many parts of the world, as well as famines. But this is only the first of the birth pains, with more to come. [9] "When these things begin to happen, watch out! You will be handed over to the local councils and beaten in the synagogues. You will stand trial before governors and kings because you are my followers. But this will be your opportunity to tell them about me. [10] For the Good News must first be preached to all nations. [11] But when you are arrested and stand trial, don't worry in advance about what to say. Just say what God tells you

79

at that time, for it is not you who will be speaking, but the Holy Spirit. [12] "A brother will betray his brother to death, a father will betray his own child, and children will rebel against their parents and cause them to be killed. [13] And everyone will hate you because you are my followers. But the one who endures to the end will be saved. [14] "The day is coming when you will see the sacrilegious object that causes desecration standing where he should not be." (Reader, pay attention!) "Then those in Judea must flee to the hills. [15] A person out on the deck of a roof must not go down into the house to pack. [16] A person out in the field must not return even to get a coat. [17] How terrible it will be for pregnant women and for nursing mothers in those days. [18] And pray that your flight will not be in winter. [19] For there will be greater anguish in those days than at any time since God created the world. And it will never be so great again. [20] In fact, unless the Lord shortens that time of calamity, not a single person will survive. But for the sake of his chosen ones he has shortened those days. [21] "Then if anyone tells you, 'Look, here is the Messiah,' or 'There he is,' don't believe it. [22] For false messiahs and false prophets will rise up and perform signs and wonders so as to deceive, if possible, even God's chosen ones. [23] Watch out! I have warned you about this ahead of time! [24] "At that time, after the anguish of those days, the sun will be darkened, the moon will give no light, [25] the stars will fall from the sky, and the powers in the heavens will be shaken. ²⁶ Then everyone will see the Son of Man coming on the clouds with great power and glory. ²⁷ And he will send out his angels to gather his chosen ones from all over the world—from the farthest ends of the earth and heaven. ²⁸ "Now learn a lesson from the fig tree. When its branches bud and its leaves begin to sprout, you know that summer is near. ²⁹ In the same way, when you see all these things taking place, you can know that his return is very near, right at the door. ³⁰ I tell you the truth, this generation will not pass from the scene before all these things take place. ³¹ Heaven and earth will disappear, but my words will never disappear. ³² "However, no one knows the day or hour when these things will happen, not even the angels in heaven or the Son himself. Only the Father knows. ³³ And since you don't know when that time will come, be on guard! Stay alert! ³⁴ "The coming of the Son of Man can be illustrated by the story of a man going on a long trip. When he left home, he gave each of his slaves instructions about the work they were to do, and he told the gatekeeper to watch for his return. ³⁵ You, too, must keep watch! For you don't know when the master of the household will return—in the evening, at midnight, before dawn, or at daybreak. ³⁶ Don't let him find you sleeping when he arrives without warning. ³⁷ I say to you what I say to everyone: Watch for him!"

ALABASTER | GOSPEL OF MARK

14

JESUS ANOINTED AT BETHANY

¹ It was now two days before Passover and the Festival of Unleavened Bread. The leading priests and the teachers of religious law were still looking for an opportunity to capture Jesus secretly and kill him. ² "But not during the Passover celebration," they agreed, "or the people may riot." ³ Meanwhile, Jesus was in Bethany at the home of Simon, a man who had previously had leprosy. While he was eating, a woman came in with a beautiful alabaster jar of expensive perfume made from essence of nard. She broke open the jar and poured the perfume over his head. ⁴ Some of those at the table were indignant. "Why waste such expensive perfume?" they asked. ⁵ "It could have been sold for a year's wages and the money given to the poor!" So they scolded her harshly. ⁶ But Jesus replied, "Leave her alone. Why criticize her for doing such a good thing to me? ⁷ You will always have the poor among you, and you can help them whenever you want to. But you will not always have me. ⁸ She has done what she could and has anointed my body for burial ahead of time. ⁹ I tell you the truth, wherever the Good News is preached throughout the world, this woman's deed will be remembered and discussed."

JUDAS AGREES TO BETRAY JESUS

¹⁰ Then Judas Iscariot, one of the twelve disciples, went to the leading priests to arrange to betray Jesus to them. ¹¹ They were delighted when they heard why he had come, and they promised to give him money. So he began looking for an opportunity to betray Jesus.

THE LAST SUPPER

[12] On the first day of the Festival of Unleavened Bread, when the Passover lamb is sacrificed, Jesus' disciples asked him, "Where do you want us to go to prepare the Passover meal for you?" [13] So Jesus sent two of them into Jerusalem with these instructions: "As you go into the city, a man carrying a pitcher of water will meet you. Follow him. [14] At the house he enters, say to the owner, 'The Teacher asks: Where is the guest room where I can eat the Passover meal with my disciples?' [15] He will take you upstairs to a large room that is already set up. That is where you should prepare our meal." [16] So the two disciples went into the city and found everything just as Jesus had said, and they prepared the Passover meal there. [17] In the evening Jesus arrived with the Twelve. [18] As they were at the table eating, Jesus said, "I tell you the truth, one of you eating with me here will betray me." [19] Greatly distressed, each one asked in turn, "Am I the one?" [20] He replied, "It is one of you twelve who is eating from this bowl with me. [21] For the Son of Man must die, as the Scriptures declared long ago. But how terrible it will be for the one who betrays him. It would be far better for that man if he had never been born!" [22] As they were eating, Jesus took some bread and blessed it. Then he broke it in pieces and gave it to the disciples, saying, "Take it, for this is my body." [23] And he took a cup of wine and gave thanks to God for it. He gave it to them, and they all drank from it. [24] And he said to them, "This is my blood, which confirms the covenant between God and his people. It is poured out as a sacrifice for many. [25] I tell you the truth, I will not drink wine again until the day I drink it new in the Kingdom of God." [26] Then they sang a hymn and went out to the Mount of Olives.

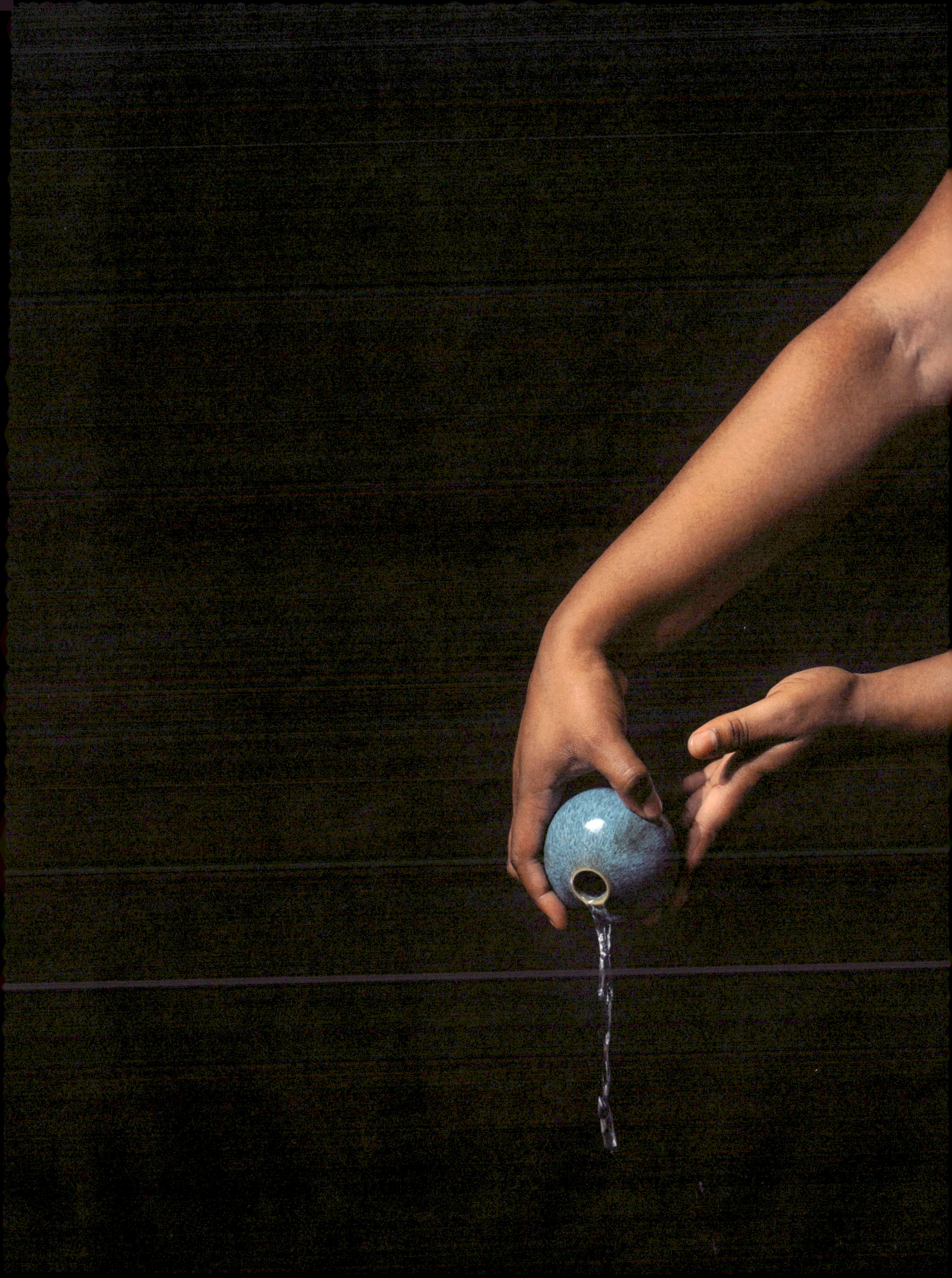

ALABASTER | GOSPEL OF MARK

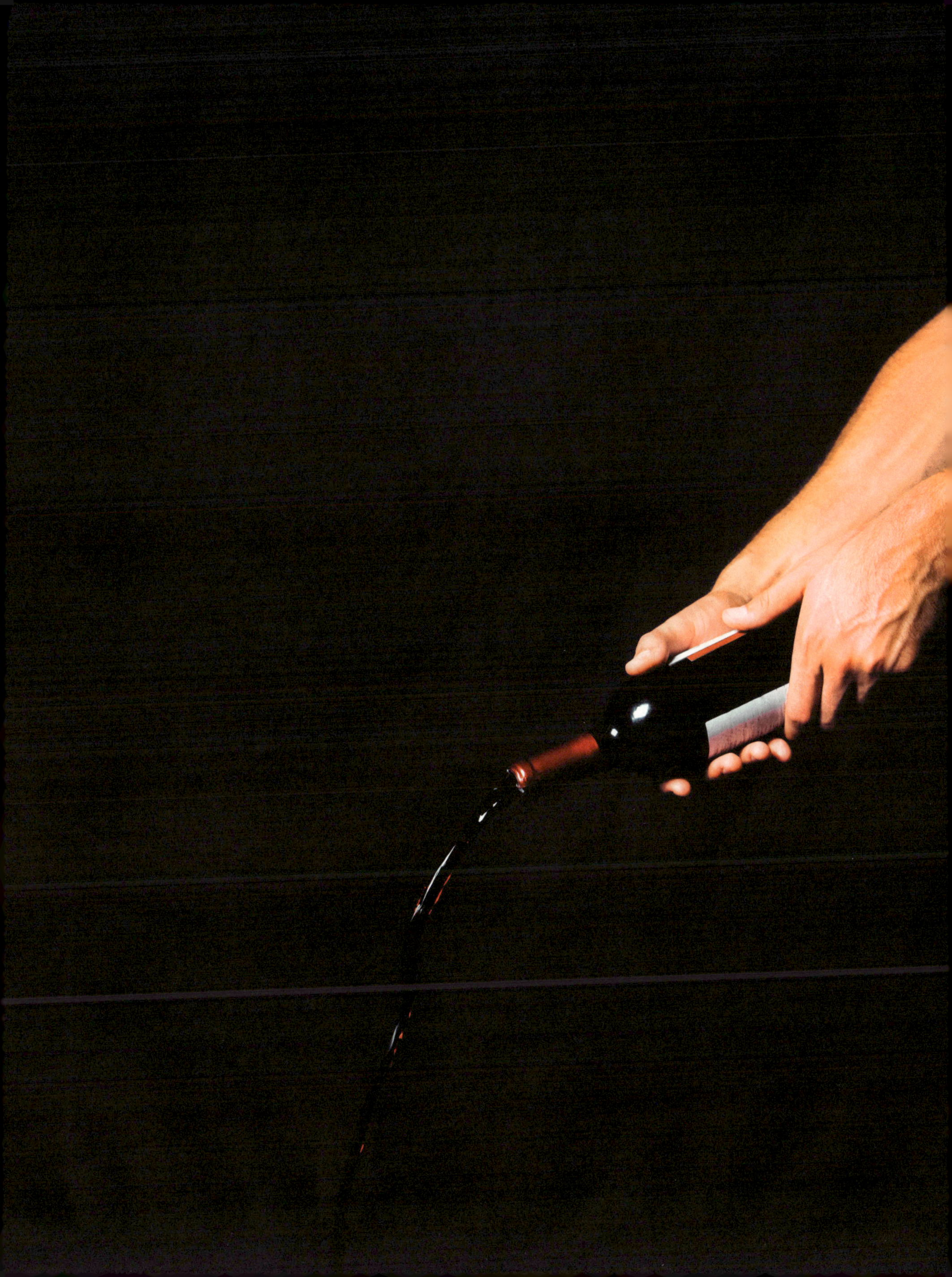

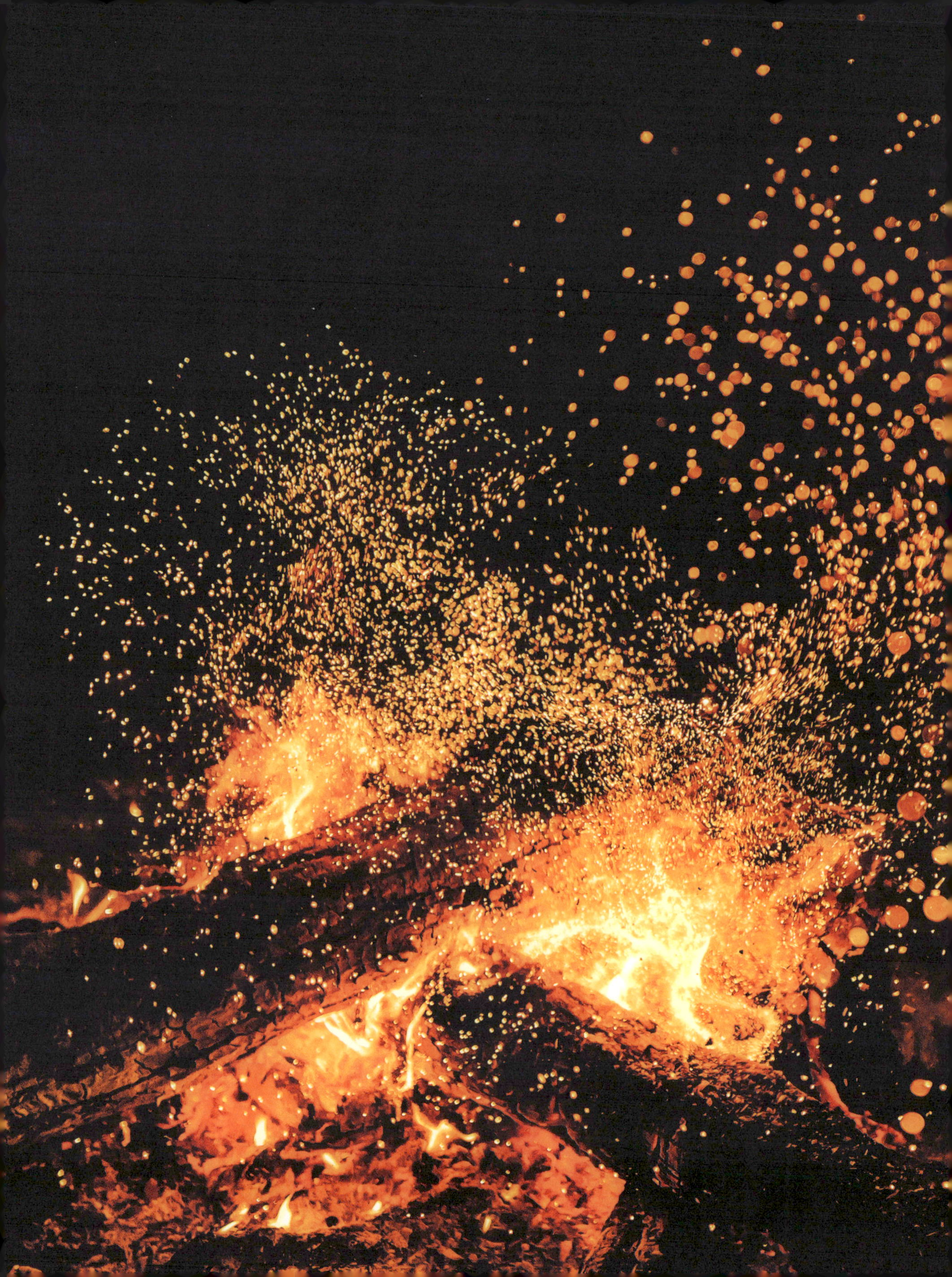

JESUS PREDICTS PETER'S DENIAL
²⁷ On the way, Jesus told them, "All of you will desert me. For the Scriptures say, 'God will strike the Shepherd, and the sheep will be scattered.' ²⁸ But after I am raised from the dead, I will go ahead of you to Galilee and meet you there." ²⁹ Peter said to him, "Even if everyone else deserts you, I never will." ³⁰ Jesus replied, "I tell you the truth, Peter—this very night, before the rooster crows twice, you will deny three times that you even know me." ³¹ "No!" Peter declared emphatically. "Even if I have to die with you, I will never deny you!" And all the others vowed the same.

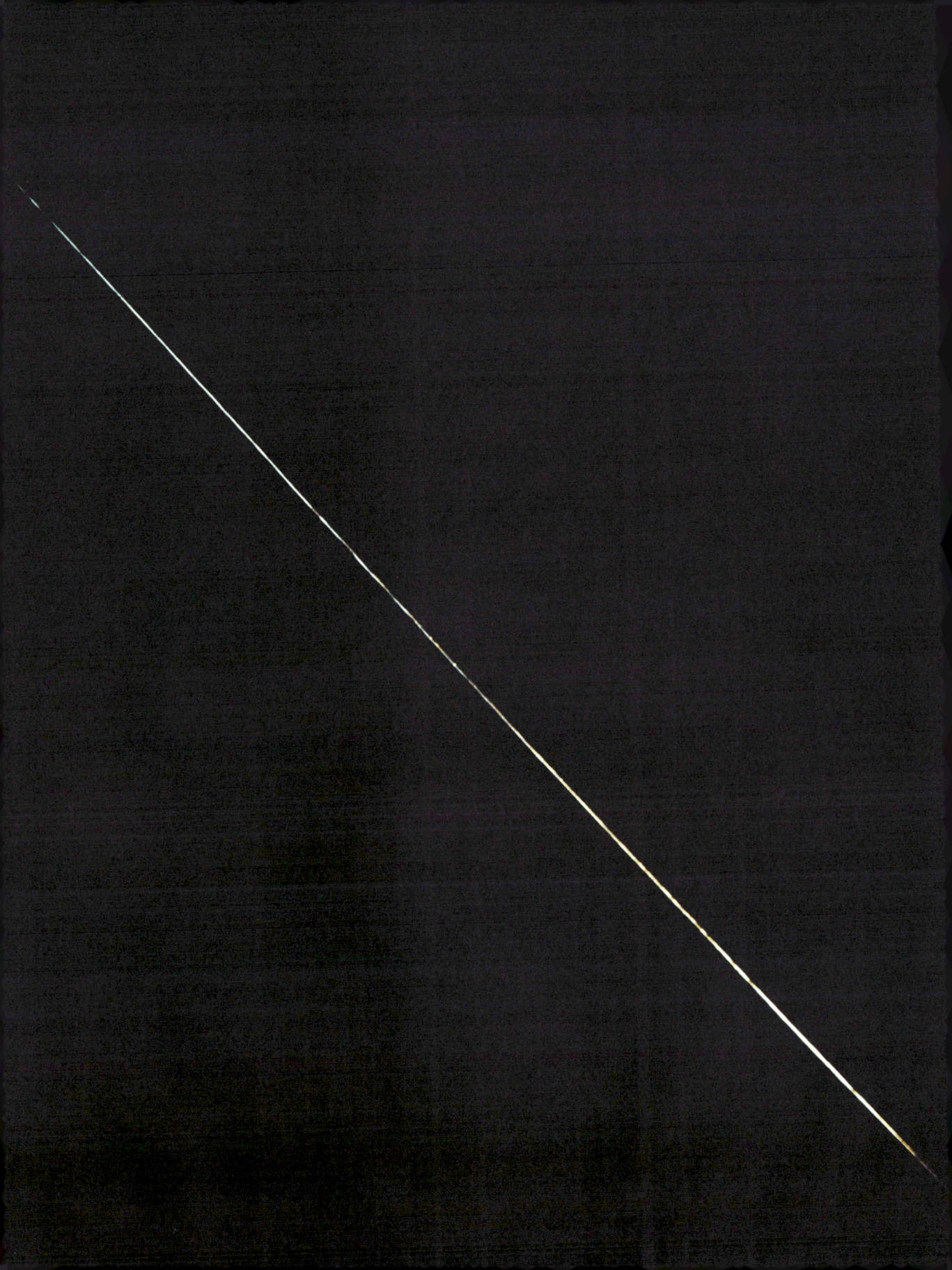

JESUS PRAYS IN GETHSEMANE

[32] They went to the olive grove called Gethsemane, and Jesus said, "Sit here while I go and pray." [33] He took Peter, James, and John with him, and he became deeply troubled and distressed. [34] He told them, "My soul is crushed with grief to the point of death. Stay here and keep watch with me." [35] He went on a little farther and fell to the ground. He prayed that, if it were possible, the awful hour awaiting him might pass him by. [36] "Abba, Father," he cried out, "everything is possible for you. Please take this cup of suffering away from me. Yet I want your will to be done, not mine." [37] Then he returned and found the disciples asleep. He said to Peter, "Simon, are you asleep? Couldn't you watch with me even one hour? [38] Keep watch and pray, so that you will not give in to temptation. For the spirit is willing, but the body is weak." [39] Then Jesus left them again and prayed the same prayer as before. [40] When he returned to them again, he found them sleeping, for they couldn't keep their eyes open. And they didn't know what to say. [41] When he returned to them the third time, he said, "Go ahead and sleep. Have your rest. But no—the time has come. The Son of Man is betrayed into the hands of sinners. [42] Up, let's be going. Look, my betrayer is here!"

JESUS IS BETRAYED AND ARRESTED

[43] And immediately, even as Jesus said this, Judas, one of the twelve disciples, arrived with a crowd of men armed with swords and clubs. They had been sent by the leading priests, the teachers of religious law, and the elders. [44] The traitor, Judas, had given them a prearranged signal: "You will know which one to arrest when I greet him with a kiss. Then you can take him away under guard." [45] As soon as they arrived, Judas walked up to Jesus. "Rabbi!" he exclaimed, and gave him the kiss. [46] Then the others grabbed Jesus and arrested him. [47] But one of the men with Jesus pulled out his sword and struck the high priest's slave, slashing off his ear. [48] Jesus asked them, "Am I some dangerous revolutionary, that you come with swords and clubs to arrest me? [49] Why didn't you arrest me in the Temple? I was there among you teaching every day. But these things are happening to fulfill what the Scriptures say about me." [50] Then all his disciples deserted him and ran away. [51] One young man following behind was clothed only in a long linen shirt. When the mob tried to grab him, [52] he slipped out of his shirt and ran away naked.

JESUS BEFORE THE COUNCIL

[53] They took Jesus to the high priest's home where the leading priests, the elders, and the teachers of religious law had gathered. [54] Meanwhile, Peter followed him at a distance and went right into the high priest's courtyard. There he sat with the guards, warming himself by the fire. [55] Inside, the leading priests and the entire high council were trying to find evidence against Jesus, so they could put him to death. But they couldn't find any. [56] Many false witnesses spoke against him, but they contradicted each other. [57] Finally, some men stood up and gave this false testimony: [58] "We heard him say, 'I will destroy this Temple made with human hands, and in three days I will build another, made without human hands.'" [59] But even then they didn't get their stories straight! [60] Then the high priest stood up before the others and asked Jesus, "Well, aren't you going to answer these charges? What do you have to say for yourself?" [61] But Jesus was silent and made no reply. Then the high priest asked him, "Are you the Messiah, the Son of the Blessed One?" [62] Jesus said, "I am. And you will see the Son of Man seated in the place of power at God's right hand and coming on the clouds of heaven." [63] Then the high priest tore his clothing to show his horror and said, "Why do we need other witnesses? [64] You have all heard his blasphemy. What is your verdict?" "Guilty!" they all cried. "He deserves to die!" [65] Then some of them began to spit at him, and they blindfolded him and beat him with their fists. "Prophesy to us," they jeered. And the guards slapped him as they took him away.

ALABASTER | GOSPEL OF MARK

PETER DENIES JESUS

⁶⁶ Meanwhile, Peter was in the courtyard below. One of the servant girls who worked for the high priest came by ⁶⁷ and noticed Peter warming himself at the fire. She looked at him closely and said, "You were one of those with Jesus of Nazareth." ⁶⁸ But Peter denied it. "I don't know what you're talking about," he said, and he went out into the entryway. Just then, a rooster crowed. ⁶⁹ When the servant girl saw him standing there, she began telling the others, "This man is definitely one of them!" ⁷⁰ But Peter denied it again. A little later some of the other bystanders confronted Peter and said, "You must be one of them, because you are a Galilean." ⁷¹ Peter swore, "A curse on me if I'm lying—I don't know this man you're talking about!" ⁷² And immediately the rooster crowed the second time. Suddenly, Jesus' words flashed through Peter's mind: "Before the rooster crows twice, you will deny three times that you even know me." And he broke down and wept.

15

JESUS' TRIAL BEFORE PILATE

[1] Very early in the morning the leading priests, the elders, and the teachers of religious law—the entire high council—met to discuss their next step. They bound Jesus, led him away, and took him to Pilate, the Roman governor. [2] Pilate asked Jesus, "Are you the king of the Jews?" Jesus replied, "You have said it." [3] Then the leading priests kept accusing him of many crimes, [4] and Pilate asked him, "Aren't you going to answer them? What about all these charges they are bringing against you?" [5] But Jesus said nothing, much to Pilate's surprise. [6] Now it was the governor's custom each year during the Passover celebration to release one prisoner—anyone the people requested. [7] One of the prisoners at that time was Barabbas, a revolutionary who had committed murder in an uprising. [8] The crowd went to Pilate and asked him to release a prisoner as usual. [9] "Would you like me to release to you this 'King of the Jews'?" Pilate asked. [10] (For he realized by now that the leading priests had arrested Jesus out of envy.) [11] But at this point the leading priests stirred up the crowd to demand the release of Barabbas instead of Jesus. [12] Pilate asked them, "Then what should I do with this man you call the king of the Jews?" [13] They shouted back, "Crucify him!" [14] "Why?" Pilate demanded. "What crime has he committed?" But the mob roared even louder, "Crucify him!" [15] So to pacify the crowd, Pilate released Barabbas to them. He ordered Jesus flogged with a lead-tipped whip, then turned him over to the Roman soldiers to be crucified.

THE SOLDIERS MOCK JESUS

[16] The soldiers took Jesus into the courtyard of the governor's headquarters (called the Praetorium) and called out the entire regiment. [17] They dressed him in a purple robe, and they wove thorn branches into a crown and put it on his head. [18] Then they saluted him and taunted, "Hail! King of the Jews!" [19] And they struck him on the head with a reed stick, spit on him, and dropped to their knees in mock worship. [20] When they were finally tired of mocking him, they took off the purple robe and put his own clothes on him again. Then they led him away to be crucified.

THE CRUCIFIXION

[21] A passerby named Simon, who was from Cyrene, was coming in from the countryside just then, and the soldiers forced him to carry Jesus' cross. (Simon was the father of Alexander and Rufus.) [22] And they brought Jesus to a place called Golgotha (which means "Place of the Skull"). [23] They offered him wine drugged with myrrh, but he refused it. [24] Then the soldiers nailed him to the cross. They divided his clothes and threw dice to decide who would get each

piece. ²⁵ It was nine o'clock in the morning when they crucified him. ²⁶ A sign announced the charge against him. It read, "The King of the Jews." ²⁷ Two revolutionaries were crucified with him, one on his right and one on his left. ²⁹ The people passing by shouted abuse, shaking their heads in mockery. "Ha! Look at you now!" they yelled at him. "You said you were going to destroy the Temple and rebuild it in three days. ³⁰ Well then, save yourself and come down from the cross!" ³¹ The leading priests and teachers of religious law also mocked Jesus. "He saved others," they scoffed, "but he can't save himself! ³² Let this Messiah, this King of Israel, come down from the cross so we can see it and believe him!" Even the men who were crucified with Jesus ridiculed him.

THE DEATH OF JESUS

³³ At noon, darkness fell across the whole land until three o'clock. ³⁴ Then at three o'clock Jesus called out with a loud voice, "Eloi, Eloi, lema sabachthani?" which means "My God, my God, why have you abandoned me?" ³⁵ Some of the bystanders misunderstood and thought he was calling for the prophet Elijah. ³⁶ One of them ran and filled a sponge with sour wine, holding it up to him on a reed stick so he could drink. "Wait!" he said. "Let's see whether Elijah comes to take him down!" ³⁷ Then Jesus uttered another loud cry and breathed his last. ³⁸ And the curtain in the sanctuary of the Temple was torn in two, from top to bottom. ³⁹ When the Roman officer who stood facing him saw how he had died, he exclaimed, "This man truly was the Son of God!" ⁴⁰ Some women were there, watching from a distance, including Mary Magdalene, Mary (the mother of James the younger and of Joseph), and Salome. ⁴¹ They had been followers of Jesus and had cared for him while he was in Galilee. Many other women who had come with him to Jerusalem were also there.

THE BURIAL OF JESUS

⁴² This all happened on Friday, the day of preparation, the day before the Sabbath. As evening approached, ⁴³ Joseph of Arimathea took a risk and went to Pilate and asked for Jesus' body. (Joseph was an honored member of the high council, and he was waiting for the Kingdom of God to come.) ⁴⁴ Pilate couldn't believe that Jesus was already dead, so he called for the Roman officer and asked if he had died yet. ⁴⁵ The officer confirmed that Jesus was dead, so Pilate told Joseph he could have the body. ⁴⁶ Joseph bought a long sheet of linen cloth. Then he took Jesus' body down from the cross, wrapped it in the cloth, and laid it in a tomb that had been carved out of the rock. Then he rolled a stone in front of the entrance. ⁴⁷ Mary Magdalene and Mary the mother of Joseph saw where Jesus' body was laid.

ALABASTER | GOSPEL OF MARK

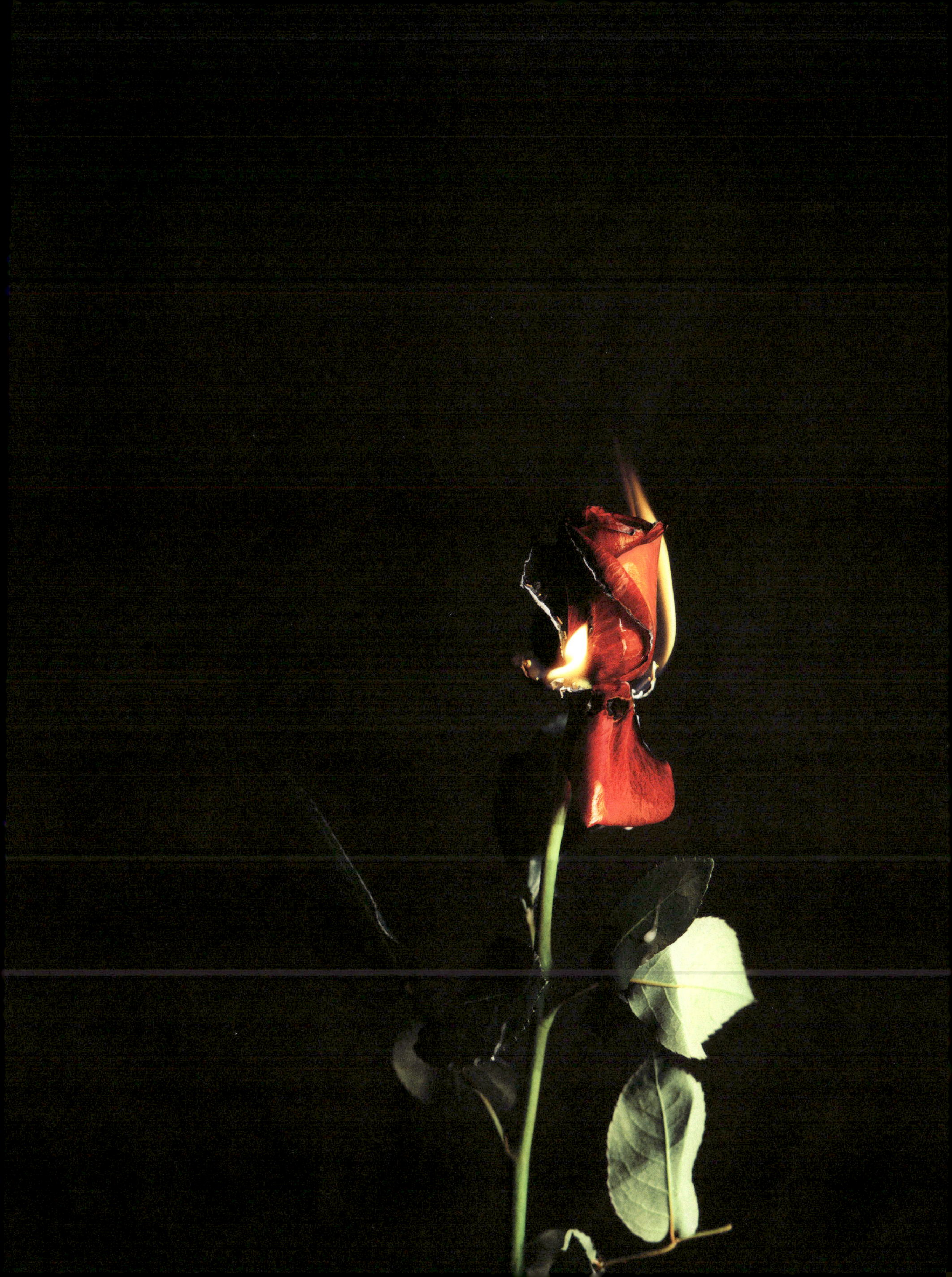

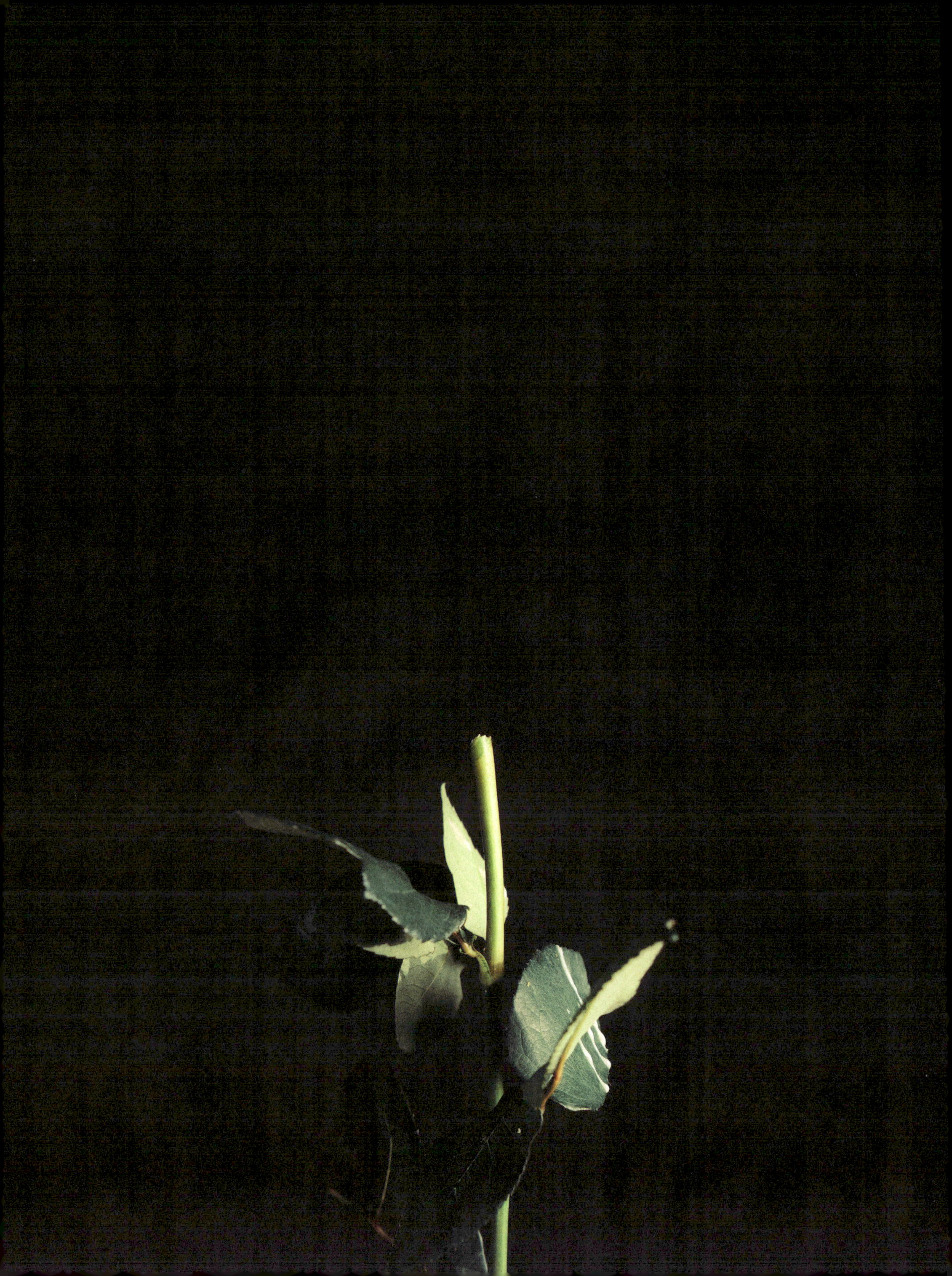

CHAPTER 15

ALABASTER | GOSPEL OF MARK

16

THE RESURRECTION

¹ Saturday evening, when the Sabbath ended, Mary Magdalene, Mary the mother of James, and Salome went out and purchased burial spices so they could anoint Jesus' body. ² Very early on Sunday morning, just at sunrise, they went to the tomb. ³ On the way they were asking each other, "Who will roll away the stone for us from the entrance to the tomb?" ⁴ But as they arrived, they looked up and saw that the stone, which was very large, had already been rolled aside. ⁵ When they entered the tomb, they saw a young man clothed in a white robe sitting on the right side. The women were shocked, ⁶ but the angel said, "Don't be alarmed. You are looking for Jesus of Nazareth, who was crucified. He isn't here! He is risen from the dead! Look, this is where they laid his body. ⁷ Now go and tell his disciples, including Peter, that Jesus is going ahead of you to Galilee. You will see him there, just as he told you before he died." ⁸ The women fled from the tomb, trembling and bewildered, and they said nothing to anyone because they were too frightened.

ALABASTER

BRYAN CHUNG
Editor in Chief & Creative Director

BRIAN CHUNG
Art Director & Business Operations

JOSEPHINE LAW
Lead Designer

IVAN BLANCO
Logo Designer

PATRON
William Pelster

PHOTOGRAPHERS
Jacob Chung
Ryan Tsuzaki

MODELS
Dani Chang
Daniel Davis
Kelechi Emetuche
Chris Miller
Sian Ye

CONTINUE THE CONVERSATION
www.alabasterco.com